I0748863

TRANSACTIONS

of the

American Philosophical Society

Held at Philadelphia for Promoting Useful Knowledge

VOLUME 82, Part 1, 1992

On Calculating the Factor of Chance in Language Comparison

DONALD A. RINGE, JR.
Associate Professor of Linguistics
University of Pennsylvania

THE AMERICAN PHILOSOPHICAL SOCIETY

Independence Square, Philadelphia

1992

Copyright © 1992 by The American Philosophical Society

Library of Congress Catalog
Card Number: 92-70402
International Standard Book Number 0-87169-821-8
US ISSN 0065-9746

for my parents

Contents

0. Introduction.

The consensus of opinion among mainstream historical linguists is that while all human languages are likely to be genetically related, the remoter relationships cannot be demonstrated by reliable linguistic methods because the languages in question have diverged too much.[1] From time to time this conventional wisdom is challenged by scholars who claim to have demonstrated one or more remote relationships; recent challenges include GREENBERG 1987 and SHEVOROSHKIN 1989. The purpose of this paper is to provide an objective test of the validity of such challenges.

Any demonstration of a relationship between languages depends largely on finding words and grammatical affixes of systematically similar shape[2] and at least roughly equivalent meaning in the languages in question. But if such a demonstration is to be convincing, one must show that the similarities adduced could not have arisen by chance. Unfortunately the possibility of chance resemblances is often dismissed without adequate discussion, apparently because common sense suggests that there is very little likelihood of words in different languages being strikingly similar in both form and meaning as a result of sheer chance.

Yet in this case common sense is wrong. The elementary mathematics of probabilities shows that any pair of languages can be expected to exhibit a non-negligible number of fortuitous similarities.[3] That is common knowledge among traditional historical linguists, and several articles on the subject have been published by competent statisticians. ROSS 1950:19-26 explored the theoretical aspects of the problem fairly thoroughly, though in highly condensed form;

---

[1] I am very grateful to Sheila Embleton for much helpful criticism of an earlier draft of this paper, for alerting me to several very important references, and for sending me copies of EMBLETON 1986 and VILLEMIN 1983; I would also like to thank Robert Oswalt for sending me a copy of his paper. I am likewise grateful to Jared Diamond, Ives Goddard, Eric Hamp, Henry Hoenigswald, Tony Kroch, Victor Mair, and Sally Thomason for helpful criticism, to Jay Jasanoff and Jerry Packard for invaluable help with the mathematics, and to Mary Ann Marcinkiewicz for checking my calculations. All remaining errors and infelicities are my own.

[2] By the shape of a linguistic form I mean the sequence of distinctive sounds (phonemes) of which it is composed; "systematically similar" refers to recurrent "matchings" of sounds, as discussed in section 2 and exemplified throughout this paper. What is important in such matchings is not that the forms in question be similar in some absolute sense, but that a substantial number of forms show exactly the same degree of similarity—or of dissimilarity (cf. ROSS 1950:20); hence the qualification "systematic". Admittedly the use of "similar" to describe such a situation is a bit misleading; but here and in various other places I have been at pains to avoid the more familiar terms "regularly corresponding" and "recurrent sound correspondence" because of their technical meaning in traditional historical linguistics. For further discussion of the latter see especially the end of section 4.

[3] OSWALT 1970:117 (in his abstract) observes that "with remotely related languages the number is never inconsequential, as is often assumed."

OSWALT 1970 proposed an original method and developed an appropriate computer program for investigating specific cases; VILLEMIN 1983 tested the methods of Ross and Oswalt in a brief exploration of some possible genetic relationships of Japanese.[4]

This monograph will address the practical aspects of the problem of chance resemblances in greater detail than any previous study known to me. My mathematical approach is much less sophisticated than those of my predecessors; indeed, I wish to emphasize that only the most elementary probability theory is needed to address the problem. I have concentrated my attention on the application of the theory to the details of particular cases for two reasons. In the first place, I have tried to keep the relation of facts to analysis as straightforward and perspicuous as possible, in the hope that my presentation can be understood both by linguists with little mathematical training and by statisticians with little knowledge of linguistic structure. More importantly, I hope to show that the structure of wordlists and the phonological structure of languages in general have profound effects on the occurrence of chance resemblances, effects which have too often been ignored.[5]

I will begin by discussing strictly limited, tightly controlled types of similarity between words, because those are easiest to understand and analyze; then I will methodically broaden my investigation to consider more complex cases.

Using the methods illustrated here, one can calculate the degree of similarity that two or more languages can be expected to show by chance alone, and also whether the similarities adduced as a demonstration of some particular linguistic relationship are significantly greater than those expected by chance; the latter calculation will constitute an objective evaluation of the claim that a relationship has been demonstrated.

[4] I am grateful to Sheila Embleton for these references. Other articles on the subject are much less useful; for further discussion see immediately below, and cf. section 1 and the end of section 5 with footnotes. Most other applications of mathematics to problems in historical linguistics are attempts to determine the closeness of relationship of two languages whose relationship has already been demonstrated beyond question; see EMBLETON 1986 with references.

[5] See especially section 1 and the end of section 5. The result of ignoring these factors is the lack of realism noted in CAMPBELL 1988:596 fn. 2; as far as I can see, FODOR 1982:80-96, JUSTESON and STEPHENS 1980, BENDER 1969, and the earlier works cited by Bender all suffer from this shortcoming to one degree or another.

1. Properties of vocabulary lists.

The most efficient way to discover systematic similarities between languages is to compare parallel basic vocabularies of the languages in question;[6] the most efficient way to arrange those vocabularies for comparison is to assign to each meaning a fixed position in the list, so that the word in any language's list that bears that meaning will always occupy that position. Such lists have well-defined structural properties, which we must understand if we are to evaluate the significance of similarities found using comparative lists.

In any language the relation between meaning and sound is largely arbitrary (ROSS 1950:19).[7] Virtually all exceptions fall into three categories:

a) "nursery words" of the type *papa, mama,* etc., which are very widespread in a great variety of language families;

b) onomatopoeic words, such as English *pow, zing,* and the like, which attempt to mimic real-world sounds;

c) series of words which, while not precisely onomatopoeic, nevertheless participate in "sound symbolism", such as the English verbs *clash, clang, clatter,* etc., all expressing violently noisy action, or *snout, sniff, sneeze, snore,* etc., all having referents connected with the nose.

These exceptions to the principle of arbitrariness should be excluded from comparative vocabulary lists, since languages which are otherwise very dissimilar are likely to exhibit similar nursery words or onomatopoeic words or systems of

[6] As is well known, it is advisable to use basic words of minimal cultural content because they are least likely to have been borrowed from other languages; greater-than-chance systematic similarities between the basic vocabularies of languages therefore usually demonstrate a genetic relationship between the languages rather than a relationship of borrowing. Similarities between grammatical affixes are also of the greatest importance; see section 10 for further discussion.

[7] This is one of the fundamental observations of fact on which scientific linguistics is built; de Saussure expressed it as *l'arbitraire du signe*. It is very easy to show the arbitrariness of the sound–meaning relation using a standard example, the word for 'horse'. In English this word begins with *h* (*horse*, phonemically /hors/); in Dutch it begins with *p* (*paard* /pa:rt/); in Welsh it begins with *m* (*march* /marx/); in French it begins with a palatoalveolar fricative (*cheval* /Šəval/); in Russian it begins with a velarized *l* (*lóšad'* /łóšat'/); in Farsi it begins with a vowel (*asp* /æsp/), and so on. There is no phonetic property that all these sounds have in common, except that they are sounds of human language made with the airstream mechanism that is overwhelmingly the most common in human language (air passing outward from the lungs); therefore we must conclude either (a) that there is no "natural" way of beginning a word meaning 'horse'—that is, no way that is dictated by the meaning of the word—or else (b) that there is a natural way to begin such a word, but that languages are perfectly free to ignore it (in which case we might ask what evidence there could possibly be for a non-arbitrary relationship between the meaning 'horse' and the sounds that express it). I am told that some who profess to study the origins of human language deny that sound–meaning relationships are arbitrary; in my opinion they are perversely denying a verifiable fact.

sound symbolism, and it might be supposed that that could skew the results of their comparison.[8]

If such exceptions are duly excluded from the lists, the relation between sound and meaning for each word in the list of each language will be arbitrary. It follows that if the list is arranged according to semantic rather than formal principles—that is, if the words are listed in some fixed order of meanings rather than ordered according to their shape in some one language—then the distribution of sounds throughout the vocabulary list of any one language will exhibit no discoverable pattern; for all practical purposes it will be random.[9] Furthermore, since the pattern of sound-to-meaning matchings in each language is effectively random, comparison of words of the same meaning in different languages should reveal a random pattern of matchings between the sounds of the two languages, except to the extent that real historical connections between the languages have given rise to similarities.[10]

However, the randomness of these patterns of sounds is not unbounded; it operates within the following constraints. In the first place, each language possesses an idiosyncratic inventory of distinctive sounds (phonemes), and also an idiosyncratic set of rules governing how those sounds can be arranged within a word

---

[8] Sheila Embleton (p. c.) points out that these exceptions constitute a tiny proportion of the vocabulary of any language, and an even smaller percentage of its basic vocabulary; therefore the danger of distortion is probably more apparent than real. I discuss them here only because they have attracted so much attention in the past. Note that the problem is not quite the same for each class of exceptions. A handful of nursery words of very similar shapes tend to reappear in large numbers of languages between which no other connection can be demonstrated. The range of onomatopoeic word-shapes, and also the number of onomatopoeic words in any language, are much larger, so that close sound-and-meaning matches between otherwise dissimilar languages are rarer; nevertheless they do occur (e.g. the word mimicking a rooster's crowing is likely to begin with *k*). In the third category of exceptions the situation is somewhat different. Each language has its own idiosyncratic system of sound symbolism, but the same semantic types of words tend to be sound-symbolic in many languages; therefore, if several members of a sound-symbolic semantic family are included in a comparative vocabulary list, there is some likelihood of finding a pattern of phonological similarities that is not historical in origin. For example, it is fairly easy to imagine a language in which 'sneeze', 'sniff', etc., all begin with *f;* and if several sound-symbolic words of the 'nose' family were included in the comparative vocabulary list, a comparison of English with our hypothetical language ("Hypo") would uncover a recurrent sound matching English *sn-* = Hypo *f-*. Since the best evidence for genetic relationships between languages is to be found in such systematic similarities, there is some risk that the matching *sn-* = *f-* might be misinterpreted as evidence of a genetic relationship between English and Hypo rather than as an artefact of sound symbolism.

[9] Strictly speaking, the appearance of particular sounds in particular words is not random, but depends on the history of those particular words in the language in question. But the histories of words are so complex, and the results (at any stage of the words' development) are contingent upon so many unique historical events, that the resulting patterns are indistinguishable from random patterns. For an interesting discussion of historical contingency, randomness, and related matters, see GOULD 1989:277-91.

[10] This last will be true even if the list is arranged so that the words of one language are ordered according to form (e.g. alphabetized).

(phonotactics); it is only within the limits dictated by a language's phonemic inventory and phonotactics that the random distribution of sounds operates. Thus in an English list the distribution of the glottalized velar stop /k'/ is not random: it necessarily never appears, because /k'/ is not a phoneme of English. Similarly, the distribution of the velar nasal /ŋ/ as a word-initial consonant in an English list is not random: though /ŋ/ is a phoneme of English, the phonotactics of the language specify that it may not occur word-initially, and so it fails to appear in that position.

Furthermore, in every language the phonemes do not appear equally often in any given permitted position in the word; for each permitted position, some phonemes are always much more common than others. For example, in a typical list of basic English words[11] the commonest word-initial consonant will be /s/, and between 13% and 17% of the words will begin with it; word-initial /w/ will be only about half as common (between 6% and 9% of the words used); and the rarest initial consonants will be /p v θ ð z č ǰ š ž y/, none of which will occur in more than 3% of the words in the list. (In fact, /ž/ is so rare that it might not occur in any word of a basic wordlist, though it is a permitted initial consonant of English.) Similar frequencies can be stated for the remaining initial consonants, and for each phoneme in each permitted position in an English word. Every language exhibits such a pattern of phonemic frequencies, which is language-specific and distinctive for that particular language. The random distribution of sounds in any wordlist operates within the constraints of the language's phonemic frequency distributions.

Note that in the preceding paragraph I have given examples of phonemic frequencies from basic English wordlists, not from English as a whole. I do so because of a further factor which influences the distribution of sounds in basic vocabulary lists. If the vocabulary of a language is etymologically uniform—that is, if there has been very little borrowing of words from other languages for many centuries, or if borrowing has affected all areas of the language's vocabulary to approximately the same degree—then the randomness of sound-to-meaning relationships will ensure that the frequencies of phonemes in the list will be approximately the same as in the language as a whole. On the other hand, if there has been relatively little borrowing of words into the basic vocabulary of a language, but massive borrowing into its non-basic vocabulary (cultural, technological, literary,

[11] I have tested this with lists of varying lengths from 100 words up to almost 600, constructed on semantic criteria and without reference to the shape of the words involved. Of course it would be possible to construct a list of "basic English words" in which these proportions failed to hold, if one deliberately set out to do so; but if the shapes of words are not made a criterion for inclusion in the list, and if the total number of words used does not fall below about 100, I believe that the statements made here will be true.

honorific, etc.), then there can be noticeable differences between the frequencies of phonemes in basic wordlists and in less basic words. English is precisely such a case: there are many English words beginning with /p/, for example, but few of them belong to the basic vocabulary, because most are relatively non-basic words borrowed from French or Latin. In order to avoid the difficulties that such cases create, it is important to investigate basic vocabulary lists per se, and not to assume that their structure always closely reflects the structure of the language as a whole.

These properties of vocabulary lists dramatically affect the number and distribution of sounds in lists. Those patterns of sounds, in turn, are the raw material for vocabulary comparisons between languages, and are thus the input for calculations of the number of interlanguage similarities likely to appear by chance in wordlist comparisons. Therefore the facts outlined above will be constantly relevant to the discussion that follows.

2. Calculating probabilities in a simple case.

In investigating how often resemblances between words of the same meaning in parallel lists will appear by chance we are dealing with the probability that random events will occur. Since the calculation of probabilities can be fairly involved, it seems best to start with simple, limited cases and then carefully expand the field of inquiry to include larger and more complex cases that more closely approximate real-language examples.[12] I begin with a maximally simple case that meets the following specifications.

(1) Only two languages will be compared at any one time, because random similarities are easiest to handle mathematically in pairwise comparisons. Once the properties of chance similarities have been worked out for two-language comparisons we will be in a position to investigate the simultaneous comparison of several languages (see section 9).

(2) Since any pair of human languages might exhibit a discoverable (but previously undiscovered) relationship which would be reflected in greater-than-chance similarity between their lexica, I will investigate chance similarities using pairs of artificial vocabularies. Since the pattern of sounds in a real-language vocabulary list is effectively random (see above), the pattern of sounds in the

[12] In the latter sections of this paper the data actually are complex real-language examples, which demonstrate that my methods are sufficiently realistic.

artificial lists must be randomized; I have accordingly constructed my wordlists with the aid of a table of random numbers. (In fact most of the "vocabularies" are purely abstract constructs; see below.) At a later stage comparisons between real languages will be introduced, and the results will be compared with the results obtained from comparison of artificial vocabularies (see sections 4 and 5).

(3) I shall at first confine myself to basic vocabularies of one hundred words, about the shortest length that might be expected to turn up a reasonable number of random similarities. After the mathematical properties of chance resemblance have been determined for such very short lists, longer lists will be introduced and examined (see section 6).[13]

(4) The words will be numbered, each number representing a "meaning", and only comparisons between words of the same meaning (i.e. bearing the same reference number) will be allowed. The mathematical consequences of relaxing this requirement will be addressed later (see section 7).

(5) At first only the initial consonants of the words will be compared; comparison of other sounds will be introduced later (see section 4).

(6) I insist that all matchings between sounds be exact, with no allowance for variation. Again, the mathematical consequences of relaxing this requirement will be addressed at a later stage (see section 8).

Let us suppose that we have two vocabularies, each a hundred words long, of the sort described in (1) through (4) above. Suppose further that in each vocabulary twenty of the words begin with the consonant *t*, [14] and that those twenty words are randomly distributed throughout the hundred words that constitute the vocabulary. The probability that a word in list A and the corresponding ("synonymous") word in list B will both begin with *t* is then $.2^2$, or .04. Of course that

---

[13] In glottochronological studies a list of about 200 basic words appears to be optimal, since calculations based on shorter lists are clearly much less accurate, while longer lists offer little increased accuracy in return for much greater labor; see e.g. TISCHLER 1973:97-100 and EMBLETON 1986:43-5, 66-7, and 89-93. As the discussion in section 6 will show, the same considerations do not apply to a probabilistic investigation of wordlist similarities.

[14] To some it may seem most unlikely that one-fifth of a language's most basic vocabulary could begin with the same consonant. However, experience shows that such cases are not rare. In the Swadesh hundred-word list for Turkish I find that 17 of the words begin with *k*, while 23 begin with vowels—that is, in terms of initial consonants they begin with "zero consonant" (see fn. 23). In languages with extremely small phonemic inventories, such as Polynesian languages, similarly large frequencies of word-initial occurrence are routine; thus in the famous case of Hawaiian, whose consonant inventory is restricted to /p k ʔ h m n l w/, the distribution of initial consonants in the Swadesh hundred-word basic wordlist is as follows:

Ø	20	l	11	p	8
ʔ	20	k	9	w	6
m	13	h	8	n	5

(/ʔ/ is the glottal stop, written " ' " in conventional Hawaiian orthography; on "Ø" see fn. 23.) For the wordlists in question see Appendix A.

does not mean that we expect to find precisely four such matchings in any pair of hundred-word lists; rather, given a suitably large number of pairwise comparisons of such lists, the average number of *t* : *t* matchings per list-comparison will be four, and the actual numbers will be distributed about that mean in a binomial distribution.[15] The distribution for a matching of probability .04 in pairwise hundred-word list comparisons is given in the leftmost column of table 1 (pp. 9-10); the "cumulative percentages" represent the sum of the percentage of comparisons for each number of matchings with the percentages for all lower numbers of matchings.[16]

[15] I learned this from PAULOS 1988:22-3, where the reasons for it are exceptionally well explained in commonsense terms.

[16] The distributions in this table were computed with a pocket calculator according to the formula taught in PAULOS 1988:22-3. I am grateful to Jerry Packard for checking the figures in an earlier version of this table and correcting some errors.

Table 1.

("%" = percent of comparisons in which each number of matchings appears; "cum." = cumulative percentages)

	probability .04		.035		.03	
no. mtchs.	%	(cum.)	%	(cum.)	%	(cum.)
0	1.7	(1.7)	2.8	(2.8)	4.8	(4.8)
1	7	(8.7)	10.3	(13.1)	14.7	(19.5)
2	14.5	(23.2)	18.5	(31.6)	22.5	(42)
3	19.7	(42.9)	21.9	(53.5)	22.7	(64.7)
4	19.9	(62.8)	19.2	(72.7)	17.1	(81.8)
5	16	(78.8)	13.4	(86.1)	10.1	(91.9)
6	10.5	(89.3)	7.7	(93.8)	5	(96.9)
7	5.9	(95.2)	3.7	(97.5)	2.1	(99)
8	2.9	(98.1)	1.6	(99.1)	0.7	(99.7)
9	1.2	(99.3)	0.6	(99.7)		
10	0.5	(99.8)				
	probability .025		.02		.018	
no. mtchs.	%	(cum.)	%	(cum.)	%	(cum.)
0	8	(8)	13.3	(13.3)	16.3	(16.3)
1	20.4	(28.4)	27.1	(40.4)	29.8	(46.1)
2	25.9	(54.3)	27.3	(67.7)	27	(73.1)
3	21.7	(76)	18.2	(85.9)	16.2	(89.3)
4	13.5	(89.5)	9	(94.9)	7.2	(96.5)
5	6.6	(96.1)	3.5	(98.4)	2.5	(99)
6	2.7	(98.8)	1.1	(99.5)		
7	0.9	(99.7)				
	probability .016		.014		.012	
no. mtchs.	%	(cum.)	%	(cum.)	%	(cum.)
0	19.9	(19.9)	24.4	(24.4)	29.9	(29.9)
1	32.4	(52.3)	34.7	(59.1)	36.3	(66.2)
2	26.1	(78.4)	24.4	(83.5)	21.8	(88)
3	13.9	(92.3)	11.3	(94.8)	8.7	(96.7)
4	5.5	(97.8)	3.9	(98.7)	2.6	(99.3)
5	1.7	(99.5)	1.1	(99.8)		

Table 1, continued.

probability	.01		.008		.006	
no. mtchs.	%	(cum.)	%	(cum.)	%	(cum.)
0	36.6	(36.6)	44.8	(44.8)	54.8	(54.8)
1	37	(73.6)	36.1	(80.9)	33.1	(87.9)
2	18.5	(92.1)	14.4	(95.3)	9.9	(97.8)
3	6.1	(98.2)	3.8	(99.1)	1.9	(99.7)
4	1.5	(99.7)				

probability	.004		.002	
no. mtchs.	%	(cum.)	%	(cum.)
0	67	(67)	81.9	(81.9)
1	26.9	(93.9)	16.4	(98.3)
2	5.3	(99.2)	1.6	(99.9)

It can be seen that in about 99% of pairwise comparisons the number of *t* : *t* matchings is nine or less. It follows that if we wished to propose a relationship between two languages on the basis of one recurrent word-initial consonant matching whose probability of chance occurrence was .04, we would have to demand *ten or more* examples of that matching in a hundred-word basic vocabulary list to ensure a 99% probability that our proposal was correct.[17]

That is likely to astonish those unfamiliar with random phenomena. In order to demonstrate that the above statements are correct, I devised the following test. I constructed fifteen artificial hundred-word "vocabularies", each containing twenty "words beginning with *t* ", using the table of random numbers in WOODS, FLETCHER, and HUGHES 1986:297.[18] The vocabularies are listed in table 2 (p.11).

---

[17] Of course one does not rely on a single set of word-initial consonant matchings to prove or disprove language relationships! I have limited this example to one set of word-initial correspondences only in order to make the mathematics as clear as possible.

[18] The "vocabularies" were constructed as follows. Starting at the top left of the table and reading horizontally, the first twenty two-digit numbers were read off; if there were duplicates, all copies of each duplicate except one were discarded, and the next number(s) were added to bring the total up to twenty. Those twenty two-digit numbers were taken to represent the positions (= "meanings") of words beginning with *t* in the first hundred-word list; all other positions in the list were taken to be filled by words not beginning with *t*. Then the next twenty numbers were read off for the second list, and so on. The resulting fifteen "vocabularies" are lists of twenty list-positions in which "words beginning with *t* " occur—a very limited artificial construct, but just enough to run the necessary test of the method of computing probabilities. Note that the randomness of the arrangement of positions of "words beginning with *t* " in each list accurately models the randomness with which such words should appear in a real-language list. Of course the fact that duplicates have been discarded means that the lists are not random in an absolute sense; but they are as random as possible consistent with the requirement that each list contain exactly twenty "words beginning with *t* ".

Each is identified by a letter; the positions ("meanings") of its twenty "words beginning with *t*" are listed following its identification letter, and all other positions are filled with "words not beginning with *t*".[19]

Table 2.

A: 02, 03, 04, 12, 14, 19, 26, 28, 29, 44, 45, 50, 51, 59, 62, 82, 85, 87, 88, 98.
B: 02, 06, 13, 22, 29, 33, 44, 50, 52, 58, 69, 70, 74, 76, 84, 86, 88, 90, 95, 98.
C: 04, 07, 20, 22, 26, 27, 47, 49, 50, 51, 52, 53, 55, 57, 59, 69, 74, 75, 90, 97.
D: 03, 11, 12, 16, 20, 21, 31, 44, 47, 53, 54, 56, 59, 70, 75, 76, 77, 89, 91, 95.
E: 01, 11, 14, 19, 22, 23, 24, 29, 30, 40, 41, 45, 47, 51, 59, 60, 75, 91, 94, 98.
F: 03, 14, 15, 16, 23, 24, 29, 35, 40, 43, 44, 46, 54, 61, 62, 66, 69, 71, 82, 91.
G: 01, 23, 27, 28, 29, 32, 36, 52, 61, 64, 65, 71, 76, 78, 80, 87, 89, 93, 97, 99.
H: 10, 12, 17, 26, 27, 28, 38, 41, 52, 64, 70, 72, 73, 76, 78, 82, 91, 93, 96, 97.
I: 09, 13, 16, 19, 20, 22, 30, 39, 40, 43, 50, 54, 56, 60, 61, 72, 81, 82, 83, 89.
J: 06, 11, 17, 19, 25, 27, 29, 30, 32, 34, 37, 41, 50, 54, 61, 69, 71, 76, 86, 99.
K: 19, 21, 22, 24, 30, 39, 40, 44, 54, 56, 63, 73, 74, 76, 87, 88, 89, 91, 97, 99.
L: 11, 17, 19, 23, 26, 48, 51, 55, 62, 66, 74, 75, 79, 81, 84, 88, 92, 96, 98, 100.
M: 09, 14, 20, 21, 22, 23, 30, 34, 39, 46, 50, 58, 63, 75, 77, 78, 81, 83, 91, 95.
N: 03, 19, 25, 44, 49, 50, 51, 57, 58, 64, 66, 70, 71, 73, 80, 82, 83, 85, 88, 93.
O: 02, 16, 17, 18, 33, 38, 42, 49, 51, 55, 60, 66, 76, 77, 80, 88, 93, 95, 96, 99.

Comparison of each of these vocabularies with every other gives 105 pairwise vocabulary comparisons of (necessarily) unrelated languages. The number of "*t* : *t* matchings" for each pairwise comparison of vocabularies is given in table 3 (p. 12); table 4 is a chart of the number of vocabulary comparisons in which each number of *t* : *t* matchings appears. The percentages of this latter table—especially the cumulative percentages—correlate strongly with those in the first column of table 1, supporting the claim that vocabulary matchings do behave in the probabilistic manner outlined above.

---

[19] The two-digit sequence "00" of the random number table has been interpreted as three-digit "100" for the purposes of these "vocabularies".

Table 3.

	A	B	C	D	E	F	G	H	I	J	K	L	M	N
B	6													
C	5	6												
D	4	5	5											
E	7	3	5	5										
F	6	3	1	5	6									
G	3	3	3	2	3	4								
H	4	3	4	4	2	2	8							
I	3	3	3	5	5	6	2	2						
J	3	6	3	3	5	5	7	4	5					
K	4	5	3	7	6	5	5	4	8	5				
L	6	4	5	2	6	3	1	3	2	3	3			
M	2	4	4	6	6	4	2	2	8	3	6	3		
N	8	5	4	3	2	5	4	5	4	4	4	4	3	
O	3	5	3	4	2	2	4	5	2	3	3	6	2	6

Table 4.

no. of mtchs.	no. of comp.	percentage	cumul. no.	cumul. percentage
0	0	0	0	0
1	2	1.9	2	1.9
2	15	14.3	17	16.2
3	26	24.8	43	41
4	20	19	63	60
5	21	20	84	80
6	14	13.3	98	93.3
7	3	2.9	101	96.2
8	4	3.8	105	100

Table 1 (pp. 9-10 above) also gives binomial distributions for some chance matchings of probability less than .04. (Chance matchings of greater probability are encountered less often.) Distributions not given in table 1 can often be estimated from those that are given; those that cannot be so estimated will be calculated as necessary below.

3. Comparisons of whole vocabularies.

Comparison of real-language vocabularies differs from the simplified example given above in that all the possible matchings of initial consonants, and of all other sounds too, are taken into consideration. Therefore we need to explore the mathematical consequences of comparing entire vocabularies (cf. ROSS 1950:19-20, 23-5).

Our procedures will be clearest if we expand the scope of our inquiry one step at a time. For the moment I will continue to consider only initial consonants in hundred-word vocabularies, but I will treat all the discoverable matchings of initial consonants in a pair of hundred-word lists. In order to do that I need actual randomized hundred-word vocabularies, or at least lists of a hundred initial consonants constructed with the help of random number tables. I have constructed six such lists of initial consonants.[20] Three of them (set A) consist of randomly distributed English consonants in the same frequencies of occurrence as the initial consonants of the English words in the standard Swadesh hundred-word list (a basic vocabulary often used for interlinguistic comparisons of various kinds).[21] In other words, since ten of the English words in the Swadesh hundred-word list begin with *b,* ten *b* 's occur in each list of set A, but the *b* 's are otherwise randomly distributed, so that there is no actual connection with the real English words; and so on. The other three lists (set B) are similar, but the consonants and their relative frequencies are

---

[20] The lists were constructed using the random number table in WOODS, FLETCHER, and HUGHES 1986:297 in the following manner. Two-digit numbers were read off the table in a row from left to right, or from right to left, or in a column from top to bottom, all duplicates being discarded except for the first occurrence of each number; I continued reading and discarding duplicates (moving to the next higher or lower row, or the next column to the left or right, as necessary) until the list contained exactly one example of each possible two-digit number. (I was careful to move around the table in such a way that nonrandomly similar patterns of numbers would not recur from list to list.) Then, in the A lists, the numbers 01 through 08 were replaced with Ø (see immediately below), 09 and 10 were replaced with /y/, 11 through 17 were replaced with /w/, etc., according to the fixed order of phonemes /y w r l m n p b f t d ð s k g h/ (/h/ replacing 92 through 00, the latter taking the place of three-digit 100), each phoneme being used exactly as many times as it appears word-initially in the real Swadesh hundred-word list for English; while in the B lists a similar replacement was effected using Latin phonemes in the relevant frequencies. Once again, the fact that duplicates have been discarded means that the lists are not random in an absolute sense; but they are as random as possible consistent with the requirement that the consonants of each list exhibit the relative frequencies of the word-initial consonants in the English or Latin Swadesh list respectively.

[21] The English list will be found in Appendix A. Note that I have altered the standard list in two respects: (1) I have replaced *person* with *human (being),* in accordance with my own usage, and (2) I have replaced *grease* with *fat,* since experience seems to show that exact equivalents of the latter word are easier to find in the dictionaries and glossaries available to me. Neither substitution should have any significant effect on the results of vocabulary comparisons.

those of Latin.[22]

The frequencies of the individual consonants in the A lists are the following:

s	14	l	5	y	2
b	10	m	5	ð	2
h	9	t	5	p	1
Ø[23]	8	k	5		
n	8	r	4		
f	8	d	4		
w	7	g	3		

(Note that not all the permitted initial consonant phonemes of English occur word-initially in the Swadesh hundred-word list.) For the B lists the frequencies are:

Ø	22	w	6	y	2
k	14	d	5	b	2
s	9	l	4	t	2
m	8	f	4	g	1
n	8	r	3		
p	7	h	3		

Since the lists were randomly constructed, all matchings between consonants will necessarily be the result of chance; but since the consonants have the same frequencies of occurrence as in the English and Latin lists respectively, the results of any comparison of an A-list with a B-list should otherwise have the properties of an English/Latin comparison. In other words, the results should be what we *would* get if English and Latin were completely unrelated languages.

Comparing each A-list with each B-list, we have nine pairwise comparisons of the "word-initial consonants" of entire hundred-word "vocabularies". I will report and discuss here the results of comparing list A-1 with list B-1; the results of the other eight comparisons, which are similar, are given in Appendix C.

We can only evaluate the results of a pairwise list comparison by checking the actual numbers of matchings found against the probability that each matching

---

22 The Latin list, too, can be found in Appendix A.

23 Included here are all words beginning with vowels. It would be possible to list the occurring initial vowels and diphthongs separately, but in that case we would be dealing with first-syllable vowels, not with initial consonants; in terms of initial consonants these words begin with "zero-consonant". Note also that listing initial vowels and diphthongs on a par with initial consonants would imply that the phonological structure of words is simply linear—i.e., that there is no phonological structure other than the sequence of phonemes. But such an assumption is known to be false: languages in fact organize the sounds of a word into syllables, the beginning of a word spoken in isolation coincides with the beginning of a syllable, and the onset of a syllable—i.e., the sequence of sounds (if any) preceding the vowel nucleus—has definable properties.

will appear. The probabilities of some matchings being found are very low; for example, the probability that the single *p* in an A list will be matched with the single *g* in a B list is .0001 (one one-hundredth of one percent). The probabilities of the matchings that are most likely to appear are given in table 5, multiplied by 100 to give the average number of actual matchings that can be expected.

Table 5.

Average number of matchings expected for the more frequent consonants of the A and B lists:

		B									
		Ø	k	s	m	n	p	w	d	l	f
A	s	3.08	1.96	1.26	1.12	1.12	.98	.84	.7	.56	.56
	b	2.2	1.4	.9	.8	.8	.7	.6	.5	.4	.4
	h	1.98	1.26	.81	.72	.72	.63	.54	.45	.36	.36
	Ø	1.76	1.12	.72	.64	.64	.56	.48	.4	.32	.32
	n	1.76	1.12	.72	.64	.64	.56	.48	.4	.32	.32
	f	1.76	1.12	.72	.64	.64	.56	.48	.4	.32	.32
	w	1.54	.98	.63	.56	.56	.49	.42	.35	.28	.28
	l	1.1	.7	.45	.4	.4	.35	.3	.25	.2	.2
	m	1.1	.7	.45	.4	.4	.35	.3	.25	.2	.2
	t	1.1	.7	.45	.4	.4	.35	.3	.25	.2	.2
	k	1.1	.7	.45	.4	.4	.35	.3	.25	.2	.2
	r	.88	.56	.36	.32	.32	.28	.24	.2	.16	.16
	d	.88	.56	.36	.32	.32	.28	.24	.2	.16	.16

The expected ranges of variation for each matching can be found by consulting table 1 (pp. 9-10 above). For example, the A : B matching s : Ø has a probability of occurrence of .0308. Table 5 tells us that we expect to find about three such matchings in an A : B list comparison on the average; finding the closest approximation among the probabilities listed in table 1, namely .03, we find that the actual numbers of matchings likely to appear in any one A : B comparison range from zero up to about eight, and that we must demand more than seven matchings to exclude chance resemblance with a probable correctness of 99%. Approximate ranges of variation for the other possible matchings can be found in the same way.

Comparison of lists A-1 and B-1 yields the actual numbers of matchings given in table 6. This table includes the likelier matchings covered in table 5, plus the three remaining matchings that appear more than once. Matchings that appear only once can be ignored, since each instance of matching is a unit event, and any unit event, no matter how improbable, can occur once by chance (cf. ROSS 1950:21).

Table 6.

Actual numbers of matchings found in the comparison of A-1 with B-1:

A-1 \ B-1	Ø	k	s	m	n	p	w	d	l	f
s	2	2	0	1	4	0	2	0	0	1
b	3	0	0	2	1	0	0	1	0	0
h	4	1	0	1	1	1	0	1	0	0
Ø	0	3	0	0	0	2	1	0	1	0
n	1	1	2	1	1	0	0	1	1	0
f	2	1	3	0	0	1	0	1	0	0
w	1	0	1	1	0	1	1	0	1	0
l	2	0	1	0	0	0	1	0	0	1
m	0	1	1	0	0	1	1	0	0	1
t	2	1	0	0	0	0	0	0	0	0
k	1	2	0	0	0	0	0	0	0	0
r	1	0	0	1	0	1	0	0	0	1
d	0	1	0	0	1	0	0	0	1	0

Note also the following less likely recurrent matchings:

y : Ø	2	(expected average number .44)
b : h	2	(expected average number .3)
k : r	2	(expected average number .15)

Note that it is important to include *all* recurrent matchings in the tables, not merely matchings of sounds that resemble one another phonetically (ROSS 1950: 20). In the normal course of natural language change, sound changes can accumulate to produce radical changes in pronunciation within a few centuries. Recurrent matchings between such sounds are no less significant than matchings between sounds that have remained more or less unchanged, and all must be treated on an equal footing. In order not to overlook possible matchings between radically changed sounds, we must investigate all recurrent matchings impartially.

Most of the numbers of matchings found fall comfortably within their expected ranges. Those that fall close to the top of their expected ranges are the following:

the 3 examples of Ø : k fall in the 89th percentile of the range expected for that matching, and
the 2 exx. of Ø : p likewise;
the 2 exx. of y : Ø fall in the 92nd;
the 3 exx. of f : s fall in the 96th percentile, and
the 2 exx. of b : h likewise;
the 4 exx. of s : n fall in the 97th;
the 2 exx. of k : r fall in the 99th.[24]

It may seem surprising to find so many matchings near the upper limit of their ranges in one list, but in fact that is what we should expect. Table 1 indicates, for each probability of occurrence of a matching, numbers of matchings so high that they will appear by chance only once in every ten instances (the 90th percentile), or twenty (the 95th), or a hundred (the 99th). But the "instances" in question are not whole list comparisons, because table 1 was not constructed with list comparisons in view; rather, a number of matchings that falls in the 99th percentile will appear by chance once in about a hundred different sound-matchings. The average number of different matchings that appear in an A : B list comparison is about 75—in effect, 75 opportunities for unusually high numbers of matchings to appear by chance. Since 75 is three-quarters of 100, we might expect a number of some matching that falls in the 99th percentile of its range to appear (on the average) about three times in every four list comparisons; thus it is not surprising to find one such number in the comparison of A-1 with B-1. For the same reason we might expect numbers of matchings that fall in the 95th and higher percentiles of their respective ranges to appear about 15 times in every four comparisons, or about four times in each comparison (on the average).

In consequence of these facts, startlingly high numbers of matchings will appear regularly even in the comparison of hundred-word lists. Working with entire vocabularies (rather than with instances of a single matching) therefore does not allow us to admit less rigorous evidence; on the contrary, it forces us to demand *greater* rigor. If we really wish to exclude chance resemblances, we must find in a

---

[24] Five unique (non-recurrent) matchings also fall in the 90th, 91st, and 92nd percentiles of their expected chance ranges. I have calculated the relevant distributions not in table 1.

Institut für Sprachwissenschaft Universität

single list comparison several matchings that fall in the 99th percentile of their expected ranges.

To investigate chance similarities between whole words, we can extend the method used above in dealing with initial consonants. Matchings of each type of phoneme in each potential position in the word must be dealt with separately in order to keep the calculation of probabilities manageable; thus we consider matchings between the initial consonants of the two languages under investigation, matchings of their first-syllable vowels, matchings of the first consonants after first-syllable vowels, and so on. Difficulties can be expected to arise if the phonotactics of the languages are very different, or if one language has lost certain sounds without a trace (see section 4 ad fin.); but because languages are idiosyncratic in these regards, such problems will have to be addressed on an ad hoc basis. In particularly difficult cases several different analyses can be attempted, and the same calculations can be performed for each.[25] I have tested this with a pair of randomly constructed artificial vocabularies, but the test revealed no methodological principles that could not be deduced from the experiments discussed above. I therefore leave the exemplification of whole-word comparisons for the following section, where data from natural languages are introduced.

4. Real-language examples: closely related languages.

If we wish to see how the above method works under maximally natural conditions, we must apply it to comparisons of natural human languages. I begin with a comparison of (standard American) English and (standard High) German, two languages which are closely and obviously related, in order to highlight the difference between random interlanguage similarities and similarities that reflect a genetic relationship. For the moment I will continue to use Swadesh hundred-words lists; the lists for these two languages can be found in Appendix A.

In the English and German hundred-word lists, word-initial consonants are distributed as follows:

[25] On the other hand, phonetic criteria for matching sounds (of the sort proposed in OSWALT 1970:118-20) should be avoided, not only because they tend to eliminate the recurrent but relatively dissimilar matchings found between remotely related languages (such as the famous correspondence Sanskrit *dv-* = Armenian *erk-*), but also because they introduce a different and mathematically incommensurable factor into the calculation.

English initial consonants:

s	14	w	7	d	4
b	10	l	5	g	3
h	9	m	5	y	2
Ø	8	t	5	ð	2
n	8	k	5	p	1
f	8	r	4		

German initial consonants:

f	11	k	7	m	4
Ø	9	z	7	t	3
h	9	r	5	c	3
b	8	l	5	d	2
v	8	n	5	p̂[26]	1
š	8	g	5		

Table 7 (pp. 20-1) lists the probabilities of initial-consonant matchings, multiplied by 100 to give an "expected chance average" number for each different matching. I have listed all possible matchings, not just those involving the commonest initial consonants, for reasons which will become clear below.

26 I use the phonemic symbol /p̂/ for the affricate [pf].

Table 7.

Expected chance averages, initial consonant matchings:

		German								
		f	Ø	h	b	v	š	k	z	r
Engl.	s	1.54	1.26	1.26	1.12	1.12	1.12	.98	.98	.7
	b	1.1	.9	.9	.8	.8	.8	.7	.7	.5
	h	.99	.81	.81	.72	.72	.72	.63	.63	.45
	Ø	.88	.72	.72	.64	.64	.64	.56	.56	.4
	n	.88	.72	.72	.64	.64	.64	.56	.56	.4
	f	.88	.72	.72	.64	.64	.64	.56	.56	.4
	w	.77	.63	.63	.56	.56	.56	.49	.49	.35
	l	.55	.45	.45	.4	.4	.4	.35	.35	.25
	m	.55	.45	.45	.4	.4	.4	.35	.35	.25
	t	.55	.45	.45	.4	.4	.4	.35	.35	.25
	k	.55	.45	.45	.4	.4	.4	.35	.35	.25
	r	.44	.36	.36	.32	.32	.32	.28	.28	.2
	d	.44	.36	.36	.32	.32	.32	.28	.28	.2
	g	.33	.27	.27	.24	.24	.24	.21	.21	.15
	y	.22	.18	.18	.16	.16	.16	.14	.14	.1
	ð	.22	.18	.18	.16	.16	.16	.14	.14	.1
	p	.11	.09	.09	.08	.08	.08	.07	.07	.05

Table 7, continued.

		German							
		l	n	g	m	t	c	d	p̂
Engl.	s	.7	.7	.7	.56	.42	.42	.28	.14
	b	.5	.5	.5	.4	.3	.3	.2	.1
	h	.45	.45	.45	.36	.27	.27	.18	.09
	ø	.4	.4	.4	.32	.24	.24	.16	.08
	n	.4	.4	.4	.32	.24	.24	.16	.08
	f	.4	.4	.4	.32	.24	.24	.16	.08
	w	.35	.35	.35	.28	.21	.21	.14	.07
	l	.25	.25	.25	.2	.15	.15	.1	.05
	m	.25	.25	.25	.2	.15	.15	.1	.05
	t	.25	.25	.25	.2	.15	.15	.1	.05
	k	.25	.25	.25	.2	.15	.15	.1	.05
	r	.2	.2	.2	.16	.12	.12	.08	.04
	d	.2	.2	.2	.16	.12	.12	.08	.04
	g	.15	.15	.15	.12	.09	.09	.06	.03
	y	.1	.1	.1	.08	.06	.06	.04	.02
	ð	.1	.1	.1	.08	.06	.06	.04	.02
	p	.05	.05	.05	.04	.03	.03	.02	.01

The numbers of initial-consonant matchings actually found in a comparison of the English and German lists are very different; they are listed in table 8 (pp. 22-3).

Table 8.

Actual numbers of initial-consonant matchings:

		German								
		f	ø	h	b	v	š	k	z	r
Engl.	s	0	0	1	0	0	**5**	1	**6**	1
	b	1	0	0	**5**	0	1	1	0	1
	h	0	0	**6**	0	1	0	1	0	0
	ø	0	**8**	0	0	0	0	0	0	0
	n	0	0	1	0	1	0	1	0	0
	f	**8**	0	0	0	0	0	0	0	0
	w	1	1	0	0	**4**	0	0	0	0
	l	0	0	0	1	0	0	0	0	0
	m	1	0	0	1	0	0	0	0	0
	t	0	0	0	1	0	1	0	0	0
	k	0	0	0	0	1	0	**3**	0	0
	r	0	0	0	0	1	0	0	0	**3**
	d	0	0	1	0	0	1	0	0	0
	g	0	0	0	0	0	0	0	0	0
	y	0	0	0	0	0	0	0	1	0
	ð	0	0	0	0	0	0	0	0	0
	p	0	0	0	0	0	0	0	0	0

Table 8, continued.

		German							
		l	n	g	m	t	c	d	p̂
Engl.	s	0	0	0	0	0	0	0	0
	b	0	0	1	0	0	0	0	0
	h	0	0	0	1	0	0	0	0
	Ø	0	0	0	0	0	0	0	0
	n	0	**5**	0	0	0	0	0	0
	f	0	0	0	0	0	0	0	0
	w	1	0	0	0	0	0	0	0
	l	**4**	0	0	0	0	0	0	0
	m	0	0	0	**3**	0	0	0	0
	t	0	0	0	0	0	**3**	0	0
	k	0	0	0	0	1	0	0	0
	r	0	0	0	0	0	0	0	0
	d	0	0	0	0	**2**	0	0	0
	g	0	0	**3**	0	0	0	0	0
	y	0	0	1	0	0	0	0	0
	ð	0	0	0	0	0	0	**2**	0
	p	0	0	0	0	0	0	0	1

The large boldface numbers in table 8 are numbers of recurrent matchings that fall in the 99th percentile of their expected ranges; note that there are sixteen of them. That alone would be enough to demonstrate beyond a reasonable doubt that English and German are related languages. The matchings in question are the following:

English	German	English	German
s	š	l	l
s	z	m	m
b	b	t	c
h	h	k	k
Ø	Ø[27]	r	r
n	n	d	t
f	f	g	g
w	v	ð	d

Since the histories of English and German, and the relationship between the two languages, have been thoroughly explored and are known in great detail, these findings can be checked against what is already known from fuller sources. In fact, all the matchings listed above reflect the real linguistic relationship between the two languages; none is the result of chance. Moreover, of the 70 word-pairs that exhibit one or another of those initial-consonant matchings, only one, the pair /beli/ : /baux/ 'belly', is a pair of completely unrelated words.[28]

In both English and German a number of words begin with clusters of two consonants, and it is also possible to compare the second consonants of these clusters. If we recognize a position for a second word-initial consonant in the phonotactics of both languages, we can list the frequencies of those second members of initial clusters that do occur and assign to all other words a "Ø" for that phonotactic slot.[29] The frequencies of occurrence of second consonants of word-initial clusters in the lists are the following:

---

27 It may seem surprising to match Ø with Ø, but such a matching follows from the considerations discussed in fn. 23; it is valid both linguistically and mathematically. In effect, I am arguing that vowel-initial words in the English list are translated by vowel-initial words in the German list more often than one might expect by chance alone. Readers who remain uneasy about this can regard Ø : Ø matchings as an example of the "lumping" of similar sounds explored in section 8; but it must be noted that I do *not* ignore the differences between the initial vowels—they are treated immediately below in the investigation of first-syllable vowels.

28 In a couple of other cases the relationship is not completely straightforward. For example, in the pair /eg/ : /ai/ 'egg' the English word was actually borrowed from Old Norse, but the Old Norse word is itself cognate with German /ai/.

29 There are other ways to organize this comparison. For example, in both languages only certain initial consonants can be followed by a second consonant; therefore we might exclude all words beginning with consonants that could not be followed by another consonant (as well as all vowel-initial words), and consider only the remaining words. I tried to do just that, but an unforeseen difficulty interfered: not every English word that begins with a consonant that could be cluster-initial is translated by a German word that begins with a consonant that could be cluster-initial, and vice versa. Apparently we must include in our calculation all words that begin with a consonant that could be cluster-initial in English *or* in German (but not in neither), or else we must include all the words in the list; and the latter course seemed less likely to introduce a bias of any sort.

English		German	
Ø	80	Ø	76
l	7	l	7
r	5	r	7
t	3	t	4
m	2	v	4
w	1	n	2
y[30]	1		
k	1		

The expected chance averages for matchings of these consonants are given in table 9, and the numbers of matchings actually found are in table 10 (p. 26).

Table 9.

Expected chance averages, second consonants of initial clusters:

		German					
		Ø	l	r	t	v	n
Engl.	Ø	60.8	5.6	5.6	3.2	3.2	1.6
	l	5.32	.49	.49	.28	.28	.14
	r	3.8	.35	.35	.2	.2	.1
	t	2.28	.21	.21	.12	.12	.06
	m	1.52	.14	.14	.08	.08	.04
	w	.76	.07	.07	.04	.04	.02
	y	.76	.07	.07	.04	.04	.02
	k	.76	.07	.07	.04	.04	.02

30 I am aware that there are good arguments for treating English /yuw/ as a phonemic unit, so that /hyuwmən/ would not begin with phonemic /hy/; however, the course adopted here seemed simpler and more straightforward for the purposes of interlanguage comparison. Adopting the alternative analysis could not cause any significant change in the results, since even under the present analysis /y/ is the second consonant of a cluster in only one word in the English list and thus cannot participate in a recurrent matching.

Table 10.

Numbers found, second consonants of initial clusters:

		German					
		Ø	l	r	t	v	n
Engl.	Ø	71	1	3	1	2	2
	l	1	**5**	0	0	1	0
	r	1	0	**4**	0	0	0
	t	0	0	0	**3**	0	0
	m	1	1	0	0	0	0
	w	0	0	0	0	1	0
	y	1	0	0	0	0	0
	k	1	0	0	0	0	0

Again, the large boldface numbers in the second table represent recurrent matchings in the 99th percentile of their expected ranges. All the word-pairs that exhibit one of these significantly recurrent matchings also exhibit one of the sixteen initial-consonant matchings listed above, and that correlation is a further indicator of the languages' relationship. (See below for further discussion of its mathematical significance.)

In contrast to initial consonants and clusters, the first-syllable vocalic nuclei of the two languages are disappointing. Readers who care to do so can find the frequencies of these nuclei, the chance probability of each matching, the expected chance average numbers of matchings in a hundred-word list comparison, and the actual numbers of matchings found, by inspecting the vocabularies in Appendix A and doing the relevant calculations. The upshot is that only three recurrent matchings fall in the 99th percentile of their expected ranges:

English æ : German a (6 found, chance average 1.35)

English i : German i (4 found, chance average .8)

English ey: German aa (3 found, chance average .4)

Since we know the history of these languages, we know that this relative lack of significantly recurring matchings has resulted chiefly from extensive changes of vowels in both languages in recent centuries. In fact, the experience of historical linguists shows that vowels and consonants are often not equally "durable" in a given language, so that for many pairs of languages the comparison either of vowels or of consonants is likely to be disappointing.[31] Note that all the word-pairs which exhibit one of these three vowel matchings also exhibit one of the sixteen initial-consonant matchings singled out above, except for /blæk/ : /švarc/ 'black', which is not a cognate pair.

We can also compare the two languages in terms of the consonant, if any, which occurs immediately after the first vocalic nucleus. The relevant consonants and their frequencies are the following:[32]

English		German	
ø	18	n	17
n	15	r	13
t	13	s	11
r	10	ø	10
l	8	l	7
d	6	t	7
m	5	g	6
k	4	x	6
θ	3	m	5
s	3	z	3
š	3	š	3
g	3	ŋ	3
ŋ	3	d	2
v	2	b	2
p	1	f	2
f	1	k	1
ð	1	c	1
z	1	p̂	1

The expected chance average numbers of matchings of these consonants are given in table 11 (pp. 28-9); the numbers of matchings actually found are given in table 12 (pp. 30-1).

[31] Among European languages the vowels are usually less useful in demonstrating relationships, but that is not true of all languages; Polynesian vowels, for example, are very stable. Eric Hamp (p. c.) suggests that the syllable structure of a language might exert considerable influence on the relative stability of its vowels and consonants.

[32] Note that in counting occurrences of the German consonants I have counted the relevant consonant of the stem, not of the word as pronounced in isolation; in practice, this means that I have ignored (or "undone") the automatic word-final devoicing of obstruents in German. I believe that such a course is by far the most realistic in terms of the structure of German; readers who do not agree can of course make the alternative choice and redo the calculations.

Table 11.

Expected chance averages, consonants immediately following the first-syllable vocalic nucleus:

		German								
		n	r	s	Ø	l	t	g	x	m
Engl.	Ø	3.06	2.34	1.98	1.8	1.26	1.26	1.08	1.08	.9
	n	2.55	1.95	1.65	1.5	1.05	1.05	.9	.9	.75
	t	2.21	1.69	1.43	1.3	.91	.91	.78	.78	.65
	r	1.7	1.3	1.1	1	.7	.7	.6	.6	.5
	l	1.36	1.04	.88	.8	.56	.56	.48	.48	.4
	d	1.02	.78	.66	.6	.42	.42	.36	.36	.3
	m	.85	.65	.55	.5	.35	.35	.3	.3	.25
	k	.68	.52	.44	.4	.28	.28	.24	.24	.2
	θ	.51	.39	.33	.3	.21	.21	.18	.18	.15
	s	.51	.39	.33	.3	.21	.21	.18	.18	.15
	š	.51	.39	.33	.3	.21	.21	.18	.18	.15
	g	.51	.39	.33	.3	.21	.21	.18	.18	.15
	ŋ	.51	.39	.33	.3	.21	.21	.18	.18	.15
	v	.34	.26	.22	.2	.14	.14	.12	.12	.1
	p	.17	.13	.11	.1	.07	.07	.06	.06	.05
	f	.17	.13	.11	.1	.07	.07	.06	.06	.05
	ð	.17	.13	.11	.1	.07	.07	.06	.06	.05
	z	.17	.13	.11	.1	.07	.07	.06	.06	.05

Table 11, continued.

		German								
		z	š	ŋ	d	b	f	k	c	p̂
Engl.	ø	.54	.54	.54	.36	.36	.36	.18	.18	.18
	n	.45	.45	.45	.3	.3	.3	.15	.15	.15
	t	.39	.39	.39	.26	.26	.26	.13	.13	.13
	r	.3	.3	.3	.2	.2	.2	.1	.1	.1
	l	.24	.24	.24	.16	.16	.16	.08	.08	.08
	d	.18	.18	.18	.12	.12	.12	.06	.06	.06
	m	.15	.15	.15	.1	.1	.1	.05	.05	.05
	k	.12	.12	.12	.08	.08	.08	.04	.04	.04
	θ	.09	.09	.09	.06	.06	.06	.03	.03	.03
	s	.09	.09	.09	.06	.06	.06	.03	.03	.03
	š	.09	.09	.09	.06	.06	.06	.03	.03	.03
	g	.09	.09	.09	.06	.06	.06	.03	.03	.03
	ŋ	.09	.09	.09	.06	.06	.06	.03	.03	.03
	v	.06	.06	.06	.04	.04	.04	.02	.02	.02
	p	.03	.03	.03	.02	.02	.02	.01	.01	.01
	f	.03	.03	.03	.02	.02	.02	.01	.01	.01
	ð	.03	.03	.03	.02	.02	.02	.01	.01	.01
	z	.03	.03	.03	.02	.02	.02	.01	.01	.01

Table 12.

Numbers found, consonants immediately following the first-syllable vocalic nucleus:

		German								
		n	r	s	ø	l	t	g	x	m
Engl.	ø	0	3	1	**7**	0	0	4	1	1
	n	**9**	1	0	1	1	1	1	1	0
	t	0	1	**8**	0	0	1	0	2	0
	r	2	**7**	0	0	0	0	1	0	0
	l	2	0	0	0	**4**	1	0	1	0
	d	0	0	0	0	1	**3**	0	0	1
	m	1	0	0	1	0	0	0	0	**3**
	k	0	1	0	0	1	0	0	1	0
	θ	2	0	0	0	0	0	0	0	0
	s	0	0	1	0	0	0	0	0	0
	š	0	0	0	0	0	0	0	0	0
	g	1	0	1	1	0	0	0	0	0
	ŋ	0	0	0	0	0	0	0	0	0
	v	0	0	0	0	0	0	0	0	0
	p	0	0	0	0	0	0	0	0	0
	f	0	0	0	0	0	1	0	0	0
	ð	0	0	0	0	0	0	0	0	0
	z	0	0	0	0	0	0	0	0	0

Table 12, continued.

		German								
		z	š	ŋ	d	b	f	k	c	p̂
Engl.	ø	0	0	0	0	0	0	1	0	0
	n	0	0	0	0	0	0	0	0	0
	t	0	0	0	0	0	0	0	1	0
	r	0	0	0	0	0	0	0	0	0
	l	0	0	0	0	0	0	0	0	0
	d	0	0	0	0	0	0	0	0	1
	m	0	0	0	0	0	0	0	0	0
	k	0	0	0	0	0	1	0	0	0
	θ	0	0	0	1	0	0	0	0	0
	s	**2**	0	0	0	0	0	0	0	0
	š	0	**3**	0	0	0	0	0	0	0
	g	0	0	0	0	0	0	0	0	0
	ŋ	0	0	**3**	0	0	0	0	0	0
	v	0	0	0	0	**2**	0	0	0	0
	p	0	0	0	0	0	1	0	0	0
	f	0	0	0	0	0	1	0	0	0
	ð	0	0	0	1	0	0	0	0	0
	z	1	0	0	0	0	0	0	0	0

Again the large boldface numbers represent recurring matchings in the 99th percentile of their expected ranges. In this case there are eleven such matchings:

English	German	English	German
ø	ø	m	m
n	n	s	z
t	s	š	š
r	r	ŋ	ŋ
l	l	v	b
d	t		

Of the 51 word-pairs in which these matchings appear, most are already represented among the significantly high matchings of word-initial consonants. There are four new pairs, namely /wən/ : /ains/ 'one', /yuw/ : /zii/ 'you', /niy/ : /knii/ 'knee', and /yelo/ : /gelb-/ 'yellow'; the only non-cognate pair is the pronoun 'you'.

The tables for second consonants of clusters immediately after the first vocalic nucleus resemble those for second consonants of initial clusters. The frequencies of the consonants in question are as follows:

English		German	
Ø	86	Ø	74
d	6	d	8
t	3	t	4
n	2	c	4
k	2	n	2
θ	1	k	2
		b	2
		s, z, š, g: 1 each[33]	

The expected chance averages of matchings can be found in table 13, the actual numbers of matchings in table 14 (p. 33).

Table 13.

Expected chance averages, second consonants of clusters after the first vocalic nucleus:

	German							
	Ø	d	t	c	n	k	b	s, z, š, g (each)
Engl. Ø	63.64	6.88	3.44	3.44	1.72	1.72	1.72	.86
d	4.44	.48	.24	.24	.12	.12	.12	.06
t	2.22	.24	.12	.12	.06	.06	.06	.03
n	1.48	.16	.08	.08	.04	.04	.04	.02
k	1.48	.16	.08	.08	.04	.04	.04	.02
θ	.74	.08	.04	.04	.02	.02	.02	.01

33 Of course the /-s/ of German /ains/ is an inflectional ending, but that cannot be seen from the list alone; consequently I treat it here as though it were part of the root.

Table 14.

Numbers found, second consonants of clusters after the first vocalic nucleus:

		German							
		Ø	d	t	c	n	k	b	s, z, š, g
Engl.	Ø	71	3	2	3	1	1	2	1s, 1z, 1š
	d	2	**3**	1	0	0	0	0	0
	t	0	0	1	1	0	0	0	1g
	n	1	0	0	0	1	0	0	0
	k	0	1	0	0	0	1	0	0
	θ	0	1	0	0	0	0	0	0

None of the recurrent matchings is found in the 99th percentile of its range. However, d : d falls just below the 99th percentile;[34] since it seems probable that that is significant, I have marked it in boldface in table 14. All three examples occur in word-pairs that are also represented above.

A final comparison can be made between the remainders of words—in effect, the second syllables minus any syllable-initial consonants (which have just been dealt with separately). It is possible to do this because English and German are so closely related that the phonotactics of these syllables are very similar (e.g. in all the words in the hundred-word list they are unstressed). However, before making this comparison we must eliminate recurrent final syllables that are obviously grammatical inflections, because a single inflection recurring many times will skew the results.[35] Various inflectional syllables do appear in the hundred-word list for each language, but only one appears repeatedly, namely the suffix /-ən/ that marks the infinitives of German verbs, which appears 19 times. I have therefore disregarded that suffix, counting the German verbs in question as words with no second syllable ("Ø" in the tables) because all have monosyllabic stems.[36] The fre-

---

34 More exactly, we expect two matchings or less in 98.7% of cases for a matching of this particular probability, and we here find three.

35 As Eric Hamp points out (p. c.), this problem could be avoided by listing stems rather than full words in the comparative vocabularies of inflected languages. I have chosen a more involved approach—listing full words, then pointing out the difficulties of doing so—in order to emphasize that the researcher *must* possess at least a rudimentary command of the grammar of the languages with which (s)he works.

36 The obvious alternative would be to eliminate all verbs from this calculation; but Sheila Embleton (p. c.) argues convincingly that the solution adopted is preferable, since it does not eliminate any of the relevant evidence for language relationship. (It is also much easier, since subtracting the verbs from the list reduces it to 81 items, and the binomial distributions of chance matchings must then be recalculated for a range of 81.) Note also that German verb stems can end in at least two of the unstressed syllables listed in the tables (though none of the verbs on the

quencies of the final syllables are the following:

English		German	
Ø	89	Ø	77
ər	4	ə	13
ən	3	ər	4
i	2	ən	3
o	1	əl	2
əz	1	əs	1

Table 15 gives the expected chance average numbers of the matchings; table 16 (p. 35) gives the numbers actually found.

Table 15.

Expected chance averages, final syllables:

		German					
		Ø	ə	ər	ən	əl	əs
Engl.	Ø	68.53	11.57	3.56	2.67	1.78	.89
	ər	3.08	.52	.16	.12	.08	.04
	ən	2.31	.39	.12	.09	.06	.03
	i	1.54	.26	.08	.06	.04	.02
	o	.77	.13	.04	.03	.02	.01
	əz	.77	.13	.04	.03	.02	.01

hundred-word list happens to do so); relatively basic examples are *sammeln* /zaməl-n/ 'to collect' and *dauern* /dauər-n/ 'to last'. (On the other hand, there is no possible contrast between stem-final /-ə-/ and Ø in verbs, and expected stem-final /-ən-/ appears instead as /-n-/ (e.g. in *trocknen* /trokn-ən/ 'to dry') and must therefore be counted as part of an intervocalic consonant cluster.) In the original version of this paper I adopted the alternative solution; the results were the same.

Table 16.

Numbers found, final syllables:

		German					
		Ø	ə	ər	ən	əl	əs
Engl.	Ø	72	11	0	3	2	1
	ər	0	0	**4**	0	0	0
	ən	3	0	0	0	0	0
	i	1	1	0	0	0	0
	o	1	0	0	0	0	0
	əz	0	1	0	0	0	0

Only the recurrent matching of /-ər/ with /-ər/ (in boldface in table 16) falls in the 99th percentile of its expected range; all four examples are found in word-pairs also exhibiting one of the significantly high matchings discussed above.

The probabilistic method of investigation employed here clearly provides massive evidence of the close relationship between English and German. To be sure, no one doubts that relationship; but since it was discovered and established not by the method used here, but by the "comparative method" (in the strict technical sense; see MEILLET 1925), it behooves us to investigate the relationship between the two methods of inquiry. That can be done most easily by considering how the significantly common recurrent matchings discovered above fit into the individual word-pairs of the hundred-word list.

Some 75 English/German word-pairs—fully three-fourths of the total—exhibit at least one significantly common recurrent matching of sounds. Of those, a considerable number exhibit more than one such matching; the following is a complete list of those word-pairs.

Three word-pairs exhibit four significantly common recurrent matchings each:

/sænd/ : /zand-/ 'sand' /driŋk/ : /triŋkən/ 'drink'[37]

/hænd/ : /hand-/ 'hand'

Seventeen word-pairs exhibit three such matchings (the English phonemes, sequences and zeroes that participate in the matchings are listed after each word-pair):

[37] The /k/ : /k/ correspondence is unique for its phonotactic position (though not, for example, word-initially); that is why I have left it out of account. Other similar examples will be found below.

/swim/ : /švimən/ 'swim' (s, i, m)
/star/ : /štern/ 'star' (s, t, r)
/stown/ : /štain/ 'stone' (s, t, n)
/fiš/ : /fiš/ 'fish' (all phonemes)
/fleš/ : /flaiš/ 'flesh' (f, l, š)
/fayər/ : /foiər/ 'fire' (f, Ø, ər)
/heyr/ : /haar/ 'hair' (all phonemes)
/bləd/ : /bluut/ 'blood' (b, l, d)
/æšəz/ : /ašə/ 'ashes' (Ø, æ, š)
/wotər/ : /vasər/ 'water' (w, t, ər)
/neym/ : /naamə/ 'name' (n, ey, m)
/klo/ : /klauə/ 'claw' (k, l, Ø)
/livər/ : /leebər/ 'liver' (l, v, ər)
/ræwnd/ : /rund-/ 'round' (r, n, d)
/mæn/ : /man/ 'man' (all phonemes)
/griyn/ : /grüün/ 'green' (g, r, n)
/ðæt/ : /das/ 'that' (all phonemes)

Thirty-five word-pairs exhibit two such matchings:

/sliyp/ : /šlaafən/ 'sleep' (s, l)
/stænd/ : /šteeən/ 'stand' (s, t)
/siy/ : /zeeən/ 'see' (s, Ø)
/sit/ : /zicən/ 'sit' (s, i)
/sey/ : /zaagən/ 'say' (s, ey)
/sən/ : /zonə/ 'sun' (s, n)
/feðər/ : /feedər/ 'feather' (f, ər)
/fut/ : /fuus/ 'foot' (f, t)
/flay/ : /fliigən/ 'fly' (f, l)
/ful/ : /fol/ 'full' (f, l)
/horn/ : /horn/ 'horn' (h, r)
/hart/ : /herc/ 'heart' (h, r)
/hiyr/ : /höörən/ 'hear' (h, r)
/hat/ : /hais/ 'hot' (h, t)
/brest/ : /brust/ 'breast' (b, r)
/bayt/ : /baisən/ 'bite' (b, t)
/ol/ : /alə/ 'all' (Ø, l)
/iyr/ : /oor/ 'ear' (Ø, r)
/iyt/ : /esən/ 'eat' (Ø, t)
/ərθ/ : /eerdə/ 'earth' (Ø, r)
/wət/ : /vas/ 'what' (w, t)
/wayt/ : /vais/ 'white' (w, t)
/nuw/ : /noi/ 'new' (n, Ø)
/kəm/ : /komən/ 'come' (k, m)
/kowld/ : /kalt/ 'cold' (k, l)
/loŋ/ : /laŋ/ 'long' (l, ŋ)
/læws/ : /lauz-/ 'louse' (l, s)
/red/ : /root/ 'red' (r, d)
/muwn/ : /moond-/ 'moon' (m, n)
/giv/ : /geebən/ 'give' (g, v)
/gud/ : /guut/ 'good' (g, d)
/tuw/ : /cvai/ 'two' (t, postvocalic Ø)
/təŋ/ : /cuŋə/ 'tongue' (t, ŋ)
/dray/ : /trokən/ 'dry' (d, r)
/ðis/ : /diizəs/ 'this' (ð, s)

Altogether, then, we find 55 word-pairs in which two or more significantly common sound-matchings occur in the same word; that is, there is a lexical correlation between significantly common matchings. This correlation is itself significant, and its significance can be expressed in mathematical terms.

Consider the English/German word-pairs that show significantly common sound-matchings both for their initial consonants and for their first-syllable vocalic nuclei. There are only twelve such words:

/æšəz/ : /ašə/ 'ashes'
/driŋk/ : /triŋkən/ 'drink'
/fiš/ : /fiš/ 'fish'
/heyr/ : /haar/ 'hair'
/hænd/ : /hand-/ 'hand'
/mæn/ : /man/ 'man'
/neym/ : /naamə/ 'name'
/sænd/ : /zand-/ 'sand'
/sey/ : /zaagən/ 'say'
/sit/ : /zicən/ 'sit'
/swim/ : /švimən/ 'swim'
/ðæt/ : /das/ 'that'

The eleven significantly common different matchings of consonants immediately *following* the first-syllable vocalic nucleus (see above) account for 51 of the postvocalic consonants and zeroes in the whole list-comparison of English and German. If those 51 sound-matchings were randomly distributed throughout the list, there would be no correlation between them and sound-matchings in earlier parts of the word; the probability that one of the significantly high postvocalic matchings would appear in any of the twelve words singled out above would be .51, and since only twelve words are under consideration we would expect to find such a postvocalic matching in .51 x 12 = 6.12 words, on the average, by chance alone. An indefinitely large number of cases would again show a binomial distribution, and the distribution over a range of 12 for an event of .51 probability is given in table 17.

Table 17.

Binomial distribution over 12 for probability .51:

no. of matchings	% expected by chance	cumulative %
0	.02	.02
1	.24	.26
2	1.37	1.63
3	4.75	6.38
4	11.13	17.51
5	18.53	36.04
6	22.5	58.54
7	20.08	78.62
8	13.06	91.68
9	6.04	97.72
10	1.89	99.61
11	.36	99.97
12	.03	100

Of the twelve word-pairs under consideration, ten exhibit significantly common postvocalic sound-matchings (the exceptions are 'say' and 'sit'). As table 17 shows, that is a number of matchings greater than we would expect to find by chance in 97.7% of all instances. By itself that result might not be high enough to invite unqualified confidence; considering the impressive findings for individual matchings, however, this lexical correlation between matchings can reasonably be called good supporting evidence for the relationship of English to German.

The same calculation can be done for various combinations of factors, always considering significantly common matchings in one particular position in the word in terms of similarly significant matchings in some other position, and in each case comparing the numbers of matchings found with the expected chance range. In general, the results are not nearly as impressive as they are for individual sound-matchings, but they are substantial enough to be used as supporting evidence.

Thus we are working with two separate sets of nonrandom distributions: the nonrandom distribution of individual sound-matchings throughout the lists, and the tendency of nonrandomly frequent matchings to cluster in the same word-pairs. These two distributions offer independent support for the relationship of languages, and the appearance of both in a single list comparison is strong evidence for linguistic relationship.

It is in the context of these findings that one can best appreciate the tremendous power of the comparative method. That method *as traditionally practiced*[38] demands the following as evidence for language relationship:

1) a relatively small number[39] of regular correspondences between the sounds of words of identical structure and meaning in different languages, each correspondence recurring many times;
2) numerous word-pairs (or word-sets, if more than one language is being compared), each of which contains examples of several regular correspondences, and a large percentage of which exhibit no other sound-matchings.

The evidence for language relationship is reckoned to improve as the number of examples of each correspondence increases and as the length of words exhibiting only regular correspondences increases, provided the number of regular correspond-

[38] For example, as practiced by mainstream Indo-Europeanists or Algonkianists or Bantuists, and (crucially) *not* as practiced by many who attempt long-range language comparisons.

[39] All the quantitative terms used in this statement of criteria are relative; traditional historical linguistics relies on the experience and judgment of its practitioners, rather than on quantitative tests, for the evaluation of hypotheses of relationship.

ences does not also increase. Irregularities of form and meaning, unique sound correspondences, etc. can be tolerated in this method, but *only* in the context of a relatively large number of word-pairs that conform strictly to the above standards.[40]

Thus the comparative method, if it is applied rigorously enough, actually works simultaneously with the two types of nonrandom distributions that are the foundation of the probabilistic method outlined here. Linguists who use the comparative method conscientiously are able to dispense with a separate calculation of probabilities because a realistic awareness of chance resemblances is implicit in the caution with which they use the comparative method and the high standards of proof which they demand. Conversely, an inexact or careless use of the comparative method does not necessarily guarantee that the results will meet the relevant standards of probability.

Moreover, once we have demonstrated a relationship between languages by probabilistic analysis, the comparative method enables us to go beyond the results of that analysis. Several of the English/German word pairs are cases in point. In the pair /driŋk/ : /triŋkən/ 'drink', only the first four phonemes of each word participate in sound-matchings which are significantly common for their respective positions in the word. Yet the matching /k/ : /k/ does recur in the English/German list comparison—it is significantly common word-initially. The solid mathematical grounding of the traditional comparative method (or, alternatively, an explicit probabilistic analysis like that undertaken above) gives us the confidence to extend our hypotheses beyond what is immediately demonstrable by probabilistic argument, and to identify the /k/ : /k/ of 'drink' with initial /k/ : /k/, treating them all as valid examples of the sound correspondence /k/ : /k/, and thus as part of the evidence for the relationship between English and German. The fact that I have been obliged to define "positions in a word" rigidly in order to develop mathematically sound probability arguments likewise obscures several significant facts about word-pairs. For example, anyone can see that the pairs of final consonants in /nat/ : /nixt/ 'not' and /nayt/ : /naxt/ 'night' are parallel; but in order to avoid "cheating", I resolved to compare English /t/ with German /x/ in both cases, since those are the immediately postvocalic consonants, thus obscuring the parallelism. The comparative method, however, enables us to set up a recurrent correspondence /t/ : /xt/, and to use that correspondence in extending our comparison of English and German; in

[40] This last point is crucial. Several of my colleagues have hastened to point out that the use of semantically inexact matchings (e.g. German *Hund* 'dog' = English *hound*), the recognition of unique (i.e. non-recurrent) sound correspondences, etc., are important parts of the traditional comparative method, and so they are; but in terms of mathematical proof those are weaknesses in the method, not strengths.

this case too, then, the comparative method allows us the freedom to find real patterns in the data once the relationship between the languages has been demonstrated.

In short, strict probabilistic demonstration of greater-than-chance resemblance between languages and the flexibility of the traditional comparative method neatly complement one another.[41] A probabilistic demonstration of language relationship (either by adherence to traditional guidelines or by explicit calculation) is always necessary, but the comparative method enables us to arrive at trustworthy results that do not proceed directly from probabilistic work.

5. Real-language examples: languages not closely related.

In this section I will apply the probabilistic method to the following pairs of languages:

a) English and Latin, two languages whose relationship is readily demonstrable but not particularly close;

b) English and Turkish, two languages generally believed not to be demonstrably related;

c) English and Navajo, two languages almost universally believed not to be demonstrably related.[42]

The Swadesh hundred-word lists for these languages can be found in Appendix A.

The frequencies of word-initial consonants in the English and Latin hundred-word lists can be found on page 14; table 5 (p. 15) gives expected chance average values for the matchings of those initial consonants. The actual comparison of English and Latin word-initial consonants is reported in table 18 (pp. 41-2).

---

[41] The same can be said of the use of other mathematical methods in historical linguistics; cf. EMBLETON 1986:168-70 with references.

[42] In (b) and (c) I exclude incidental borrowings of words as a result of recent contact. Such borrowings are not numerous, even between English and Navajo (which are in intimate contact), and none have entered the languages' basic vocabularies; for example, English has borrowed from Navajo only words denoting Navajo cultural artefacts (e.g. 'hogan'), while speakers of Navajo normally avoid foreign vocabulary even in reference to recently imported items, almost always preferring "loan translation" or some other use of native resources to coin new words.

Table 18.

Numbers found, word-initial consonant matchings:

		Latin								
		Ø	k	s	m	n	p	w	d	l
Engl.	s	0	1	**5**	0	1	1	1	2	1
	b	4	1	1	3	0	0	1	0	0
	h	1	**6**	0	1	0	0	0	0	0
	Ø	**6**	1	0	0	0	0	0	0	0
	n	0	1	1	0	**5**	0	0	0	0
	f	2	1	0	0	0	**4**	1	0	0
	w	4	1	0	1	1	0	0	0	0
	l	0	0	0	0	0	1	0	0	1
	m	1	0	0	2	0	0	1	0	1
	t	1	1	0	0	0	0	0	2	1
	k	2	0	0	0	1	0	1	0	0
	r	0	0	0	0	0	1	0	0	0
	d	0	1	1	1	0	0	0	0	0
	g	0	0	0	0	0	0	1	1	0
	y	0	0	0	0	0	0	0	0	0
	ð	1	0	0	0	0	0	0	0	0
	p	0	0	1	0	0	0	0	0	0

Table 18, continued.

		Latin f	r	h	y	b	t	g
Engl.	s	1	0	1	0	0	0	0
	b	0	0	0	0	0	0	0
	h	0	0	1	0	0	0	0
	Ø	0	0	0	0	0	1	0
	n	0	0	0	0	0	0	1
	f	0	0	0	0	0	0	0
	w	0	0	0	0	0	0	0
	l	1	0	0	**2**	0	0	0
	m	0	0	0	0	0	0	0
	t	0	0	0	0	0	0	0
	k	1	0	0	0	0	0	0
	r	0	**3**	0	0	0	0	0
	d	0	0	0	0	1	0	0
	g	0	0	0	0	1	0	0
	y	1	0	0	0	0	1	0
	ð	0	0	1	0	0	0	0
	p	0	0	0	0	0	0	0

The large boldface numbers are numbers of recurrent matchings that fall in the 99th percentile of their expected chance ranges. Note that there are only seven of them, and that together they represent only 31 word-pairs. That is far fewer than in the case of English and German, and it shows that English and Latin are not nearly so closely related. The matchings and word-pairs in question are the following:

s : s /siyd/ : /sēmen/ 'seed'
/sit/ : /sedēre/ 'sit'
/stænd/ : /stāre/ 'stand'
/sən/ : /sōl/ 'sun'
/star/ : /stēlla/ 'star'

r : r /ruwt/ : /rādīks/ 'root'
/red/ : /ruber/ 'red'
/ræwnd/ : /rotundus/ 'round'

n : n /nat/ : /nōn/ 'not'
/nowz/ : /nāsus/ 'nose'
/nayt/ : /nokt-/ 'night'
/nuw/ : /nowos/ 'new'
/neym/ : /nōmen/ 'name'

l : y /livər/ : /yekur/ 'liver'
/lay/ : /yakēre/ 'lie'

h : k /huw/ : /kwis/ 'who'
/horn/ : /kornū/ 'horn'
/heyr/ : /kapillus/ 'hair'
/hed/ : /kaput/ 'head'
/hart/ : /kord-/ 'heart'
/hat/ : /kalidus/ 'hot'

f : p /fiš/ : /piskis/ 'fish'
/feðər/ : /penna/ 'feather'
/fut/ : /ped-/ 'foot'
/ful/ : /plēnus/ 'full'

Ø : Ø /ay/ : /ego/ 'I'
/ol/ : /omnēs/ 'all'
/eg/ : /ōwom/ 'egg'
/iyr/ : /auris/ 'ear'
/ay/ : /okulus/ 'eye'
/iyt/ : /edere/ 'eat'

Since Latin, too, is a language whose history and relationships are thoroughly known, we can judge these matchings against wider and more exact knowledge. Most of the words are in fact related in one way or another, though the relationship is not always one of exact cognation; for example, English /red/ and Latin /ruber/ are descended from different derivatives of the same Proto-Indo-European root, while the ancestor of English /ræwnd/ was actually borrowed from a descendant of Latin /rotundus/. (The probabilistic method does not help the researcher to recover the morphological history of a word, and it is quite unable to distinguish between cognation and borrowing; these are significant drawbacks of the method.) But five of these pairs—namely 'hair', 'hot', 'liver', 'lie', and 'all'—contain completely unrelated words, and their initial sound-matchings are the result of chance. Moreover, those chance pairs include both examples of the recurrent initial matching l : y, whose very existence is thus the result of chance. That so much random "noise" intrudes on our comparison of English and Latin likewise shows that the languages are not very closely related.

Initial consonant clusters are also found in Latin, though not as often as in English or German. The frequencies of second-position consonants in English and Latin are as follows:

English		Latin	
Ø	80	Ø	91
l	7	l	3
r	5	w	2
t	3	t	2
m	2	r	1
w	1	k	1
y	1		
k	1		

Tables 19 gives the expected chance averages for matchings of these consonants, and table 20 the numbers of matchings actually found.

Table 19.

Expected chance averages, second consonants of initial clusters:

		Latin					
		Ø	l	w	t	r	k
Engl.	Ø	72.8	2.4	1.6	1.6	.8	.8
	l	6.37	.21	.14	.14	.07	.07
	r	4.55	.15	.1	.1	.05	.05
	t	2.73	.09	.06	.06	.03	.03
	m	1.82	.06	.04	.04	.02	.02
	y	.91	.03	.02	.02	.01	.01
	k	.91	.03	.02	.02	.01	.01

Table 20.

Numbers found, second consonants of initial clusters:

		Latin					
		Ø	l	w	t	r	k
Engl.	Ø	73	3	2	0	1	1
	l	7	0	0	0	0	0
	r	5	0	0	0	0	0
	t	1	0	0	**2**	0	0
	m	2	0	0	0	0	0
	y	1	0	0	0	0	0
	k	1	0	0	0	0	0

The numbers found look absolutely random, except for the matching t : t, which falls in the 99th percentile of its expected chance range. The words in question are 'stand' and 'star' (see above).

The comparison of first-syllable vowel nuclei is even more disappointing than for English and German; not one of the English/Latin matchings falls in the 99th percentile of its expected chance range. I can see no point in reporting the details here.

Consonants immediately following the first-syllable vowel nucleus yield slightly better results. It is at this point that grammatical affixes intrude on our comparison of English and Latin: the Latin infinitive ending /-re/ directly follows the first vowel of the stem in several verbs (/skīre/, /nāre/, /stāre/, /dare/), and we must discount it in order to avoid skewing the results, recognizing these verb stems as vowel-final, i.e. having "Ø" after the vowel.[43] Making that adjustment, I find that the frequencies of the relevant consonants in the two lists are as follows:

English		Latin	
Ø	18	n	19
n	15	r	16
t	13	l	10
r	10	d	10
l	8	m	8
d	6	k	8
m	5	Ø	7
k	4	s	5
θ, s, š, g, ŋ	3 each	w, g	4 each
v	2	p, t, b	3 each
p, f, ð, z	1 each		

The expected chance averages for matchings of the commoner consonants are given in table 21 (p. 46), and the numbers of matchings found in table 22.

[43] In nouns, too, I have counted the stem-final consonant, which does not always appear in the nominative singular form cited in dictionaries.

Table 21.

Expected chance averages, consonants immediately following the first-syllable vocalic nucleus:

	Latin									
	n	r	l	d	m	k	ø	s	w	g
E. ø	3.42	2.88	1.8	1.8	1.44	1.44	1.26	.9	.72	.72
n	2.85	2.4	1.5	1.5	1.2	1.2	1.05	.75	.6	.6
t	2.47	2.08	1.3	1.3	1.04	1.04	.91	.65	.52	.52
r	1.9	1.6	1	1	.8	.8	.7	.5	.4	.4
l	1.52	1.28	.8	.8	.64	.64	.56	.4	.32	.32
d	1.14	.96	.6	.6	.48	.48	.42	.3	.24	.24
m	.95	.8	.5	.5	.4	.4	.35	.25	.2	.2
k	.76	.64	.4	.4	.32	.32	.28	.2	.16	.16

Table 22.

Numbers found, consonants immediately following the first-syllable vocalic nucleus:

	Latin									
	n	r	l	d	m	k	ø	s	w	g
E. ø	2	2	1	1	0	4	3	2	1	2
n	4	3	2	0	0	0	2	1	0	0
t	1	1	3	**6**	0	2	0	0	0	0
r	0	**6**	1	1	0	0	0	0	1	0
l	3	1	0	1	1	0	0	0	1	1
d	2	0	0	0	1	0	0	0	0	0
m	1	0	1	0	2	0	1	0	0	0
k	0	0	1	0	2	0	0	0	0	0

Additional recurrent matchings:

n : t	2	ŋ : n	2
d : b	2		

The only numbers that fall in the 99th percentile of their expected chance ranges are the two in boldface. Seven of the word-pairs that contain one of those two matchings also exhibit word-initial consonant matchings that are significantly common; they are 'sit', 'horn', 'heart', 'ear', 'eat', 'foot', and 'root' (see above). The five new word-pairs are the following:

/bark/ : /korteks/ 'bark'
/wət/ : /kwid/ 'what'
/ərθ/ : /terra/ 'earth'
/fæt/ : /adeps/ 'fat'
/bərn/ : /ārdēre/ 'burn'

Of the five, only 'what' is a pair of related words; the remaining matchings are the result of chance.

The second consonants of medial clusters furnish no further matchings in nonrandomly high quantities, and the structure of English and Latin words is so different that the ends of words can scarcely be compared at all.

The results of this comparison are meager enough. We have only nine words that contain two matchings whose numbers break the 99th-percentile threshold:

/stænd/ : /stāre/ 'stand' (s, t)
/iyr/ : /auris/ 'ear' (Ø, r)
/star/ : /stēlla/ 'star' (s, t)
/iyt/ : /edere/ 'eat' (Ø, t)
/sit/ : /sedēre/ 'sit' (s, t)
/fut/ : /ped-/ 'foot' (f, t)
/horn/ : /kornū/ 'horn' (h, r)
/ruwt/ : /rādīks/ 'root' (r, t)
/hart/ : /kord-/ 'heart' (h, r)

Moreover, the lexical correlation of matchings is not very impressive. There are 31 word-pairs that exhibit significantly common initial sound-matchings, and twelve that exhibit such matchings in the position immediately after the first-syllable vocalic nucleus. Only seven word-pairs of the latter class also belong to the former—a figure that is in the 95th percentile of its expected chance range.

To be sure, the probabilistic method does demonstrate that English and Latin are related, and such a demonstration is necessary before we can embark on further meaningful comparative work. But the comparative method again enables us to find further patterns. The matching t : d, which appears to be mathematically significant only in the position after the first vowel or diphthong, also occurs initially (in /tuw/ : /duo/ 'two' and /tuwθ/ : /dent-/ 'tooth'), as well as postconsonantally (in /hart/ : /kord-/ 'heart'); the comparative method recognizes this as the regular correspondence t : d in all positions. Similarly, the regular correspondence n : n, which is very common initially and postvocalically, can also be recognized in /horn/ : /kornū/ 'horn'. Note that the last two cases provide us with examples containing three recurrent correspondences each.

This case, then, also demonstrates that the probabilistic and comparative methods complement each other, each contributing something of value.

The comparison of English and Turkish gives unusual results. The frequencies of initial consonants in the English hundred-word list are by now familiar;

the Turkish frequencies are the following:

Ø	23	b	14	t	5
k	17	d	10	g	5
y	15	s	6	č, ǰ, v, m, n	1 each

The expected chance averages of the matchings are given in table 23; table 24 (p. 49) reports the numbers of initial-consonant matchings found.

Table 23.

Expected chance averages, matchings of initial consonants (the last column giving the expected chance averages for each of the sounds č, ǰ, v, m, n):

		Turkish								
		Ø	k	y	b	d	s	t	g	č &c.
Engl.	s	3.22	2.38	2.1	1.96	1.4	.84	.7	.7	.14
	b	2.3	1.7	1.5	1.4	1	.6	.5	.5	.1
	h	2.07	1.53	1.35	1.26	.9	.54	.45	.45	.09
	Ø	1.84	1.36	1.2	1.12	.8	.48	.4	.4	.08
	n	1.84	1.36	1.2	1.12	.8	.48	.4	.4	.08
	f	1.84	1.36	1.2	1.12	.8	.48	.4	.4	.08
	w	1.61	1.19	1.05	.98	.7	.42	.35	.35	.07
	l	1.15	.85	.75	.7	.5	.3	.25	.25	.05
	m	1.15	.85	.75	.7	.5	.3	.25	.25	.05
	t	1.15	.85	.75	.7	.5	.3	.25	.25	.05
	k	1.15	.85	.75	.7	.5	.3	.25	.25	.05
	r	.92	.68	.6	.56	.4	.24	.2	.2	.04
	d	.92	.68	.6	.56	.4	.24	.2	.2	.04
	g	.69	.51	.45	.42	.3	.18	.15	.15	.03
	y	.46	.34	.3	.28	.2	.12	.1	.1	.02
	ð	.46	.34	.3	.28	.2	.12	.1	.1	.02
	p	.23	.17	.15	.14	.1	.06	.05	.05	.01

Table 24.

Numbers found, matchings of initial consonants:

		Turkish								
		Ø	k	y	b	d	s	t	g	č &c.
Engl.	s	2	2	2	0	4	0	2	2	0
	b	1	**6**	1	1	0	0	0	0	1m
	h	3	1	1	2	0	2	0	0	0
	Ø	0	2	2	2	0	0	1	1	0
	n	1	0	1	3	2	0	0	1	0
	f	4	0	1	1	1	0	1	0	0
	w	1	1	1	2	0	1	0	0	1n
	l	1	0	2	1	0	0	0	0	1ǰ
	m	3	0	0	0	1	0	0	0	1č
	t	2	1	0	0	2	0	0	0	0
	k	1	0	0	1	0	1	1	1	0
	r	0	2	2	0	0	0	0	0	0
	d	2	2	0	0	0	0	0	0	0
	g	1	0	1	0	0	0	0	0	1v
	y	0	0	0	0	0	**2**	0	0	0
	ð	1	0	0	1	0	0	0	0	0
	p	0	0	1	0	0	0	0	0	0

For the most part these numbers appear to be random, but the two boldface numbers fall in the 99th percentile of their expected chance ranges. Since we would expect to find only one such number (or none at all) by chance in most cases, we must ask whether this result might not reveal a relationship of some sort between English and Turkish.

In fact, it is easy to show that these matchings do not reveal any relationship between the languages, using purely historical arguments as follows. The word-pairs in question are the following:

/bərd/ : /kuš/ 'bird'	/beli/ : /karn-/ 'belly'
/bark/ : /kabuk/ 'bark'	/blæk/ : /kara/ 'black'
/bləd/ : /kan/ 'blood'	/yuw/ : /sen/ 'you'
/bown/ : /kemik/ 'bone'	/yelo/ : /sarɨ/ 'yellow'

None of these word-pairs can reflect borrowing (direct or mediated) between English and Turkish since at least the eighth century A.D., because since that time—and almost certainly for much longer—neither English nor Turkish has undergone sound changes drastic enough to give rise to words of such different shape. Earlier borrowing is unlikely for the same reason, and also because the languages ancestral to English and Turkish occupied widely separated parts of the globe throughout their history.[44] Therefore, if any relationship exists, it cannot have resulted from contact at any period when Germanic was a recognizable entity; it must be genetic instead—that is, some ancestor of Turkish would have to be related to the earliest reconstructable ancestor of English, Proto-Indo-European (PIE). But it is seems clear that all the English words beginning with /b/ listed above entered the language after the PIE period. The words for 'blood' and 'bone' are Germanic innovations (Proto-Germanic (PG) *blōdą and *bainą); the PIE words were *ésh$_2$r̥ and *h$_2$óst respectively. *Black* first acquired its meaning in Old English (OE); OE *blæc* is in semantic competition with *sweart,* the reflex of PG *swarta-, the usual Germanic stem. There does seem to have been a PG *blaka- as well, but its reflexes in most Germanic languages mean 'ink' (originally *'soot'?); and in any case the word is a Germanic innovation. *Belly* acquired its present meaning only in Middle English; the OE word was *wamb,* and OE *belg* meant '(leather) bag', as do all its cognates. Though there are some cognates outside of Germanic (e.g. Old Irish *bolg*), the word is confined to northern Europe and cannot be shown to have been inherited from PIE. *Bark* was borrowed from Old Norse; it is clear that the word arose within the North Germanic subgroup, thus after the PG period. *Bird* first acquired its present meaning in Middle English ('bird' in OE was *fugol,* the usual Germanic word); its OE ancestor, *bridd* 'young bird', seems to be an original English creation, as there are no certain cognates in other languages. Since none of these words was inherited from PIE, while any relationship between English and Turkish would have to be mediated by PIE, we must conclude that the initial consonant matchings of the English and Turkish words are the result of chance. As for English *you* and *yellow,* they did not begin with the same consonant in Old Eng-

[44] Specifically, the Germanic languages have occupied northern Europe since Proto-Indo-European began to diversify, while Turkic languages (other than the divergent Chuvash) are solidly attested first in the vicinity of western Mongolia. The observation that the Huns probably spoke a language of the Turkic family, while the Goths—some of whom were Hunnish vassals—spoke a Germanic language, does not invalidate my argument. In the first place, English is not a descendant of Gothic; indeed, the ancestors of the English were living on the shores of the North Sea during the period when Huns were conquering Goths in the Ukraine. More importantly, Turkish is clearly not a descendant of Hunnish; the Huns moved into the European world in the fourth century A.D. and were absorbed into other peoples in the area within a century or so, while the ancestors of the Osmanli Turks remained in Central Asia until the thirteenth century A.D.

lish (the OE forms were *ēow* and *geolu*); that they do so now is a more recent accident, and it follows that the apparent correspondence of English /y/ with Turkish /s/ is also an accident.

Thus we are forced to conclude that there is no historical relationship between the English and Turkish words, and it follows that the numbers of initial-consonant matchings found must be the result of chance. Those who care to investigate the first-syllable vocalic nuclei of English and Turkish, or the consonants that immediately follow, will discover that the matchings between them are random; that result confirms the conclusion of the above argument. The comparative method, too, concurs: traditional historical linguists who apply their method rigorously have been unable to demonstrate any relationship between the Indo-European family and the Turkic group.

I have dwelt on this case at some length because of what it reveals about our methods. A number of matchings in the 99th percentile of its expected range appears (by definition) once in every hundred matchings; and because such unusually high numbers are distributed randomly among the matchings we make between the sounds of wordlists,[45] more than one such number will occasionally appear for a single phonotactic position in a single list comparison, even though the typical list comparison involves fewer than 100 different matchings for each position. In fact, the distribution of such numbers over sets of matchings should be binomial. If each list comparison involved exactly 100 different matchings, we could simply read from table 1, column .01, how often a given 99th-percentile number of matchings might be expected to appear in a single list comparison. Since the numbers of different matchings in list comparisons are typically smaller, we must recalculate that distribution for smaller ranges; but unless the number of different matchings in a single list comparison is very small indeed, it is clear that two numbers of matchings in the 99th percentile of their expected ranges will not be remarkably high. It follows that two 99th-percentile numbers of matchings for a single phonotactic position in a single list-comparison *must not* be taken as evidence for linguistic relationship without further investigation. Random chance does not present us with such cases very often, but it does do so occasionally.

The case of English and Navajo is more straightforward. The frequencies of stem-initial consonants in the Navajo list are as follows:

[45] Except to the extent that real historical connections have given rise to similarities.

c	12	z	4	
n	8	γ	4	
d	7	y	4	
k	7	b	3	
ł	6	t	3	
t'	5	h	3	
k'	5	ǯ, g, č, ƛ', c', l, s, š, ž, Ø		2 each
ʔ	5	λ, ʒ, ƛ, m		1 each

Readers who care to do so can calculate the expected chance average numbers for matchings of English and Navajo initials; there does not seem to be much point in tabulating them here, as a glance at table 25 (p. 53) will demonstrate.

Table 25.

Numbers found, matchings of the commoner initial consonants:

		Navajo							
		c	n	d	k	ł	t'	k'	ʔ
Engl.	s	1	1	1	2	1	0	1	1
	b	2	0	1	1	0	0	0	0
	h	2	0	3	0	0	0	0	0
	Ø	0	1	0	0	2	1	0	0
	n	0	1	1	0	0	0	1	0
	f	1	0	0	2	1	2	1	0
	w	0	1	0	0	1	0	0	1
	l	0	1	0	0	0	1	0	0
	m	0	0	0	0	0	0	0	1
	t	3	1	0	0	0	0	0	0
	k	0	0	0	1	0	0	2	0
	r	0	1	0	1	0	0	0	0
	d	2	0	0	0	1	0	0	0

		Navajo					
		z	γ	y	b	t	h
Engl.	s	1	1	1	0	0	0
	b	0	1	0	2	0	0
	h	0	0	0	0	0	1
	Ø	0	0	2	0	0	0
	n	1	0	0	0	0	0
	f	0	0	0	1	0	0
	w	0	0	0	0	1	1
	l	1	0	1	0	1	0
	m	1	0	0	0	0	1
	t	0	1	0	0	0	0
	k	0	1	0	0	0	0
	r	0	0	0	0	0	0
	d	0	0	0	0	0	0

Additional recurrent matching:

s : s 2

The numbers of table 25 reflect random matchings; all are very low, and not one falls in the 99th percentile of its expected chance range. Comparison of vowels and noninitial consonants gives similar results. Thus the probabilistic method asserts unequivocally that English and Navajo are not demonstrably related. The comparative method concurs.

The real-language comparisons undertaken in this section show that the probabilistic method distinguishes well between languages whose relationship can be demonstrated by careful comparative work and languages which cannot be shown to be related. It seems clear that this approach accurately reflects the workings of chance and the laws of probability as applied to human language.

It is worth asking whether these results could not be codified in a simple formula. If we could specify some minimum number of matchings required to demonstrate a historical connection between two languages, it would then be much easier to test pairs of languages to see whether they are demonstrably related.[46] Unfortunately a careful examination of the evidence shows that such an approach, if it is possible at all, will be no easier than the detailed method exemplified here. The critical difficulty is the fact that the frequencies of occurrence of individual phonemes vary so widely, both from language to language and especially within a single language.

To illustrate this difficulty, let us attempt a comparison of Turkish and Hawaiian. The hundred-word list of the former shows thirteen different word-initial consonants (including Ø); that of the latter shows only nine (including Ø). If those consonants were evenly distributed in each list, the frequency of each Turkish initial consonant would be about .077, while that of each Hawaiian initial consonant would be .111; the probability of a matching between any two consonants would be about .0085, and four or five examples of any matching would constitute potential evidence for a relationship between the two languages (see table 1, p. 10). But in each language some word-initial consonants are much more common than others. Twenty of the Hawaiian words begin with Ø, and another twenty begin with /ʔ/; twenty-three of the Turkish words begin with Ø, and another seventeen begin with /k/. The probability of a matching between any of these initials is therefore in the neighborhood of .04, and four or five examples certainly would *not* constitute potential evidence of relationship; on the contrary, that is about the average number of matchings that we would expect by chance, far below the 99th-percentile threshold. Clearly it makes a difference which recurrent matchings we find; we cannot

---

[46] I am grateful to Jared Diamond for pointing this out.

simply require some particular number of any recurrent matching. Studies of chance resemblances which deal with the average frequencies of phonemes rather than their actual frequencies are thus easily led into error.[47]

Adding Navajo to the comparison introduces a further complication. The Navajo list shows twenty-eight different initials (including Ø); thus, even if we could average out their frequencies of occurrence without falsifying the picture, the average frequency of a Navajo initial would be only about .036—less than half the average frequency of a Turkish initial. Clearly there is no one level of overall resemblance which will be equally significant for all languages, no matter how we compute it.[48] There is no substitute for a detailed investigation of the data.

6. Lengthening the wordlists.

If we consider the pairs of languages investigated in the last two sections, it is hard to see how using longer wordlists could improve our understanding of the relationship between English and German, Turkish, or Navajo; it is too clear that English is closely related to German and not demonstrably related to the other two languages. In the comparison of English and Latin, however, it seems reasonable to ask whether the analysis of more data might lead to clearer results. Consequently I shall use English and Latin as the test languages for longer wordlists. A 200-word basic vocabulary of those two languages can be found in Appendix D.[49]

Before we begin this test, however, we must recalculate the expected ranges for chance matchings of different probabilities, since the binomial distributions of numbers of matchings will not be the same for 200-word lists as for hundred-word lists. Table 26 (pp. 56-7) gives the ranges for matchings of several different probabilities (chiefly those which will be important in the actual comparison of English and Latin).

---

47 This is one of the chief shortcomings of FODOR 1982:80-96.

48 We might at least hope that a language with as many initials as Navajo would distribute them more evenly among its basic vocabulary, but the table of frequencies on page 52 shows that we are disappointed even in that expectation.

49 This vocabulary is one version of Swadesh's 200-word list, with a few modifications. Repeated attempts to improve the list have convinced me that the one given in this paper is about as good as any.

Table 26.

probability	.03		.02		.017	
no. mtchs.	%	(cum.)	%	(cum.)	%	(cum.)
0	.23	(.23)	1.76	(1.76)	3.24	(3.24)
1	1.4	(1.63)	7.18	(8.94)	11.21	(14.45)
2	4.3	(5.93)	14.58	(23.52)	19.29	(33.74)
3	8.79	(14.72)	19.63	(43.15)	22.02	(55.76)
4	13.38	(28.1)	19.73	(62.88)	18.75	(74.51)
5	16.22	(44.32)	15.79	(78.67)	12.7	(87.21)
6	16.31	(60.63)	10.47	(89.14)	7.15	(94.36)
7	13.98	(74.61)	5.92	(95.06)	3.42	(97.78)
8	10.43	(85.04)	2.92	(97.98)	1.43	(99.21)
9	6.88	(91.92)	1.27	(99.25)		
10	4.07	(95.99)				
11	2.17	(98.16)				
12	1.06	(99.22)				

probability	.016		.012		.01	
no. mtchs.	%	(cum.)	%	(cum.)	%	(cum.)
0	3.97	(3.97)	8.94	(8.94)	13.4	(13.4)
1	12.92	(16.89)	21.72	(30.66)	27.07	(40.47)
2	20.9	(37.79)	26.25	(56.91)	27.2	(67.67)
3	22.43	(60.22)	21.04	(77.95)	18.14	(85.81)
4	17.96	(78.18)	12.59	(90.54)	9.02	(94.83)
5	11.45	(89.63)	5.99	(96.53)	3.57	(98.4)
6	6.05	(95.68)	2.37	(98.9)	1.17	(99.57)
7	2.73	(98.41)	.8	(99.7)		
8	1.07	(99.48)				

Table 26, continued.

probability	.0096		.0085		.0045	
no. mtchs.	%	(cum.)	%	(cum.)	%	(cum.)
0	14.53	(14.53)	18.14	(18.14)	40.57	(40.57)
1	28.16	(42.69)	31.1	(49.24)	36.68	(77.25)
2	27.16	(69.85)	26.52	(75.76)	16.5	(93.75)
3	17.37	(87.22)	15.01	(90.77)	4.92	(98.67)
4	8.29	(95.51)	6.34	(97.11)	1.1	(99.77)
5	3.15	(98.66)	2.13	(99.24)		
6	.99	(99.65)				

probability	.0036		.002		.0018	
no. mtchs.	%	(cum.)	%	(cum.)	%	(cum.)
0	48.61	(48.61)	67.01	(67.01)	69.75	(69.75)
1	35.13	(83.74)	26.86	(93.87)	25.15	(94.9)
2	12.63	(96.37)	5.36	(99.23)	4.51	(99.41)
3	3.01	(99.38)				

probability	.001		.0006	
no. mtchs.	%	(cum.)	%	(cum.)
0	81.86	(81.86)	88.69	(88.69)
1	16.39	(98.25)	10.65	(99.34)
2	1.63	(99.88)		

As before, I begin with the initial consonants of English and Latin. These are distributed in the lists as follows:

English initial consonants:

s	33	d	9	θ	5
f	20	r	8	y	4
w	17	l	8	p	4
Ø	16	t	7	ð	4
h	16	k	7	š	2
b	15	m	6	č	1
n	12	g	5	v	1

Latin initial consonants:

Ø	40	m	12	r	5
k	24	n	12	g	5
s	20	l	10	h	5
p	17	t	10	b	4
w	13	d	7	y	3
f	13				

Since the lists are 200 words long, the frequency of each initial consonant, expressed as a percentage of the combined incidence of all initial consonants and zeroes, can be found by dividing each of the above figures by two.

The probability of each matching occurring by chance, found by multiplying the frequencies of the consonants in question, is given in table 27 (p. 59). Table 28 (p. 60) gives the average number of matchings expected to occur by chance, found by multiplying the probabilities by 200. The actual numbers of matchings found are reported in table 29 (pp. 61-2).

Table 27.

Probabilities of matchings occurring by chance:

		Latin						
		Ø	k	s	p	w, f	m, n	l, t
Engl.	s	.033	.0198	.0165	.014025	.010725	.0099	.00825
	f	.02	.012	.01	.0085	.0065	.006	.005
	w	.017	.0102	.0085	.007225	.005225	.0051	.00425
	Ø, h	.016	.0096	.008	.0068	.0052	.0048	.004
	b	.015	.009	.0075	.006375	.004875	.0045	.00375
	n	.012	.0072	.006	.0051	.0039	.0036	.003
	d	.009	.0054	.0045	.003825	.002925	.0027	.00225
	r, l	.008	.0048	.004	.0034	.0026	.0024	.002
	t, k	.007	.0042	.0035	.002975	.002275	.0021	.00175
	m	.006	.0036	.003	.00255	.00195	.0018	.0015
	g, θ	.005	.003	.0025	.002125	.001625	.0015	.00125
	y, p, ð	.004	.0024	.002	.0017	.0013	.0012	.001
	š	.002	.0012	.001	.00085	.00065	.0006	.0005
	č, v	.001	.0006	.0005	.000425	.000325	.0003	.00025

		Latin			
		d	r, g, h	b	y
Engl.	s	.005775	.004125	.0033	.002475
	f	.0035	.0025	.002	.0015
	w	.002975	.002125	.0017	.001275
	Ø, h	.0028	.002	.0016	.0012
	b	.002625	.001875	.0015	.001125
	n	.0021	.0015	.0012	.0009
	d	.001575	.001125	.0009	.000675
	r, l	.0014	.001	.0008	.0006
	t, k	.001225	.000875	.0007	.000525
	m	.00105	.00075	.0006	.00045
	g, θ	.000875	.000625	.0005	.000375
	y, p, ð	.0007	.0005	.0004	.0003
	š	.00035	.00025	.0002	.00015
	č, v	.000175	.000125	.0001	.000075

Table 28.

Expected chance averages, initial consonant matchings:

		Latin								
		Ø	k	s	p	f, w	m, n	l, t	d	r, g, h
Engl.	s	6.6	3.96	3.3	2.805	2.145	1.98	1.65	1.155	.852
	f	4	2.4	2	1.7	1.3	1.2	1	.7	.5
	w	3.4	2.04	1.7	1.445	1.045	1.02	.85	.595	.425
	Ø, h	3.2	1.92	1.6	1.36	1.04	.96	.8	.56	.4
	b	3	1.8	1.5	1.275	.975	.9	.75	.525	.375
	n	2.4	1.44	1.2	1.02	.78	.72	.6	.42	.3
	d	1.8	1.08	.9	.765	.585	.54	.45	.315	.225
	r, l	1.6	.96	.8	.68	.52	.48	.4	.28	.2
	t, k	1.4	.84	.7	.595	.455	.42	.35	.245	.175
	m	1.2	.72	.6	.51	.39	.36	.3	.21	.15
	g, θ	1	.6	.5	.425	.325	.3	.25	.175	.125
	y, p, ð	.8	.48	.4	.34	.26	.24	.2	.14	.1
	š	.4	.24	.2	.17	.13	.12	.1	.07	.05
	č, v	.2	.12	.1	.085	.065	.06	.05	.035	.025

		Latin	
		b	y
Engl.	s	.66	.495
	f	.4	.3
	w	.34	.255
	Ø, h	.32	.24
	b	.3	.225
	n	.24	.18
	d	.18	.135

		Latin	
		b	y
Engl.	r, l	.16	.12
	t, k	.14	.105
	m	.12	.09
	g, θ	.1	.075
	y, p, ð	.08	.06
	š	.04	.03
	č, v	.02	.015

Table 29.

Numbers found, initial consonant matchings:

		Latin								
		ø	k	s	p	w	f	m	n	l
Engl.	s	3	3	**10**	2	1	3	1	2	2
	f	2	4	0	**9**	1	2	0	1	0
	w	7	2	1	0	2	0	1	1	2
	ø	**11**	1	1	0	1	0	0	0	0
	h	2	6	0	0	1	1	2	0	0
	b	4	2	2	0	1	1	4	0	0
	n	1	2	1	1	0	0	0	**6**	0
	d	0	1	2	1	0	1	1	0	0
	r	0	0	0	2	0	2	0	0	0
	l	0	0	1	1	0	1	0	0	2
	t	1	1	0	0	1	0	0	0	2
	k	2	0	1	0	1	1	0	2	0
	m	1	0	0	0	1	0	**3**	0	1
	g	1	0	0	0	1	0	0	0	0
	θ	0	2	0	0	0	0	0	0	0
	y	1	0	0	0	1	1	0	0	0
	p	0	0	1	0	0	0	0	0	1
	ð	3	0	0	0	0	0	0	0	0
	š	1	0	0	0	0	0	0	0	0
	č	0	0	0	1	0	0	0	0	0
	v	0	0	0	0	1	0	0	0	0

Table 29, continued.

		Latin						
		t	d	r	g	h	b	y
Engl.	s	1	2	1	0	1	1	0
	f	0	0	0	1	0	0	0
	w	1	0	0	0	0	0	0
	Ø	1	0	0	1	0	0	0
	h	1	0	0	1	2	0	0
	b	1	0	0	0	0	0	0
	n	0	0	0	1	0	0	0
	d	0	1	0	0	1	1	0
	r	0	1	**3**	0	0	0	0
	l	0	0	1	0	0	0	**2**
	t	0	2	0	0	0	0	0
	k	0	0	0	0	0	0	0
	m	0	0	0	0	0	0	0
	g	0	1	0	1	0	1	0
	θ	2	0	0	0	0	0	1
	y	1	0	0	0	0	0	0
	p	2	0	0	0	0	0	0
	ð	0	0	0	0	1	0	0
	š	0	0	0	0	0	1	0
	č	0	0	0	0	0	0	0
	v	0	0	0	0	0	0	0

As in the case of the hundred-word list, only seven matchings (in boldface in table 29) fall in the 99th percentile of their expected chance ranges. Six of them appear also in the hundred-word list comparison:

s : s   Ø : Ø   r : r
f : p   n : n   l : y

The last of these is entirely the result of chance; the others all include cognate pairs, and sometimes also pairs related by borrowing. (The more numerous matchings also include a chance example or two, as one might expect.) But the seventh matching, m : m, crosses the threshold of the 99th percentile only in this list. Of the three examples, 'many' is the result of chance, 'mother' is a cognate pair, and 'mountain' reflects borrowing from French (a daughter of Latin) into English. Conversely, the matching h : k, which was significantly frequent in the hundred-word list and does include some cognate pairs, falls below the 99th percentile in this comparison. It does not fall far below: there are six examples of the matching, and we expect to find five or less in 98.66% of all instances. But if we include this matching in the "significantly frequent" category, we must also include b : m, since we find four examples of that matching and expect to find three or less in 98.67% of all instances. Yet b : m includes no word-pairs that are related in any way. It seems better to take the "99th percentile threshold" seriously and exclude both these matchings.

Apparently the actual numbers of words involved are so small that random fluctuation in the identities of the words included in the lists can seriously affect the frequency of sound-matchings. But in spite of that problem the overall picture is clear: the probabilistic method gives roughly the same results with the 200-word list as with the hundred-word list. Even in commonsense terms that is not surprising. It is true that longer lists from two demonstrably related languages will include more related words, but they will also include more unrelated words, which will generate more random "noise" among the sound-matchings.[50] In addition, the expected chance ranges are broader for longer lists (compare table 26 with table 1). Readers who care to continue this experiment with the noninitial consonants will find that in those cases too the 200-word list gives no particular advantage to the researcher.

In fact, as the lists become longer a factor which tends to *decrease* the frequency of the most frequent matchings will begin to operate. As linguists have long known, basic vocabulary tends to be replaced less often than nonbasic vocabulary; in other words, in any given period of time the percentage of old nonbasic words which a language loses (and replaces with new words) will be greater than the percentage of basic words which it loses.[51] Cognates—inherited words pre-

---

[50] As Eric Hamp (p. c.) points out, other factors will also increase this "noise"; for example, in longer lists there will be more examples of historically valid but unique sound correspondences, which because of their uniqueness cannot contribute positively to a probabilistic evaluation of relationship.

[51] Of course one cannot simply divide a language's vocabulary into "basic" and "nonbasic" categories; there is a continuum of basicness, so to speak. However, the statement in the text is true modulo that complication. Note that while there is a clear correlation between "basicness" and resistance to replacement, the former need not be defined in terms of the latter; basic words can be recognized in part by frequency of usage (more basic words tend to be more frequently used) and in part by observation of their psychological content, as revealed e.g. by the use of the words in metaphors. (Thus English *hand*, for example, appears in many more metaphors and idioms than *elbow*, and the same is probably true of the corresponding words in most (all?) languages.)

served by two or more related languages—therefore tend to cluster in the basic vocabulary. As the comparative lists are lengthened, the words included will be progressively less basic on the average, since a language has only so much basic vocabulary; eventually the overall percentage of cognate pairs will drop noticeably, and unless one language has borrowed massively from the other[52] the frequency of the most frequent matchings must therefore gradually decrease until none cross the 99th-percentile threshold. Thus we can say that at best the use of longer vocabulary lists does not improve the probabilistic method.[53]

For the comparative method, however, using longer lists does confer a significant advantage. Unless the languages in question are extremely distantly related, increasing the length of the lists increases the number of cognates at one's disposal and thus makes the recognition of recurrent correspondences easier. One might suggest that a linguist investigating a possible language relationship make a probabilistic comparison with hundred-word lists and (if the results of that comparison are positive) collect much longer lists with which to find regular sound correspondences by the comparative method.

7. Comparison of approximate synonyms.

Change in the meanings of words is one of the most usual kinds of language change, and its direct consequence is that cognate words in related languages often do not translate one another. A linguist looking for cognates will therefore find it advisable to compare a given word of language X not only with its translation in language Y, but also with all other words of Y whose meanings are similar. Since that is part of the normal practice of comparative linguistics, we need to see what effect it has on the numbers of sound-matchings that are likely to occur by chance alone.

Consider the similar[54] meanings 'cheek', 'jaw', and 'chin'. Semantic shifts within this family of meanings are well attested in numerous language groups, and one would certainly expect a linguist to look for such shifts in investigating a possi-

---

[52] Rough experimentation suggests that English borrowings from French and Latin begin to have an impact on the figures as the length of the list approaches 600 words.

[53] Of course there is also a lower limit of list length, since very short lists will not contain enough words to include a significant number of cognates and borrowings; lists shorter than a hundred words do not seem to work well unless the languages are very closely related.

[54] These meanings are "similar" in that they refer to parts of the body so closely contiguous that in some real-world situations one could as well make reference to one as to another. Other types of semantic similarity are exemplified in the list of linked words below.

ble language relationship. Let us suppose, then, that all three meanings occur in some basic vocabulary list, and that a linguist investigating the possible relationship of two languages X and Y by means of such a list wishes to check all possible matchings of the three words. The relevant part of the list will have the following form:

	X	Y
'cheek'	bcd	fgh
'jaw'	jkl	mnp
'chin'	qrs	tvw,

in which the alphabetized sequences of consonants stand for the actual words of the two languages. It is clear that in order not to miss any possible cognates the linguist must compare each of the three X words with each of the three Y words; thus *bcd* will participate in three word-comparisons, as will *fgh,* and so will each of the other words.

But because *bcd* participates in three word-comparisons, its initial consonant ("*b* ") must be counted three times in computing the initial-consonant frequencies of X; if it is counted only once, the computation of the probabilities of chance matchings will be inaccurate, since two of the matchings in which *bcd* participates will be unaccounted for. The same is true of each of the other five words under consideration. For statistical purposes that amounts to adding six words to each list. It is evident that if a large proportion of words in a list are compared not only with words that translate them but also with words which do not, the effective length of the list will increase substantially. One can demonstrate the process using the hundred-word list of Appendix A. Suppose that in addition to comparing words of one language with their translations in the other we make the following reasonably plausible cross-comparisons:

'I' with 'we' (two additional comparisons, i.e. 'I' of the first language with 'we' of the second and vice versa), on the grounds that if they are made to different roots the 'first person' root to which the singular is made in one language might appear in the plural in the other;

'this' with 'that' (two additional comparisons, hereafter abbreviated "+2");

'who' with 'what' (+2);

'big' with 'long' (+2);

'man' with 'human' (+2);

'bark' with 'skin' (+2);

'feather' with 'hair' (+2);

'feather' with 'fly' (+2; but 'hair' with 'fly' is much less likely, hence I omit it);
'tooth' with 'bite' (+2);
'heart' with 'liver' (+2);
'see' with 'know' (+2);
'sleep' with 'die' (+2);
'die' with 'kill' (+2; but 'sleep' with 'kill' is much less likely);
'walk', 'come', and 'path' (+6);
'sun' with 'moon' (+2);
'water' with 'rain' (+2);
'sand' with 'earth' (+2);
'cloud' with 'smoke' (+2);
'fire', 'burn', and 'hot' (+6);
'green' with 'yellow' (+2);
'black' with 'night' (+2).

Although the number of plausible cross-comparisons is limited in so small and basic a list, I have added fifty new comparisons, effectively increasing the length of the list by half. Longer lists containing more semantically similar words would permit a higher proportion of cross-comparisons, and could double in length if many cross-comparisons were allowed.[55]

The mathematical consequences of lengthening the list in this way are the following. The expected ranges of chance matchings are larger for longer lists, so that a larger number of actual matchings would be required to cross the 99th-percentile threshold and offer potential evidence for linguistic relationship. But though the number of potential matchings is increased by semantic cross-comparisons, and that increase must be reflected in our calculations of chance matchings, the number of actual cognates does not increase (except in the infrequent cases in which a word of one language is partially cognate with two or more words in the other language). Thus in order to demonstrate nonrandom similarities one is forced to meet the statistical requirements of a longer list using the cognate resources of a shorter one—a non-negligible handicap.

---

[55] Of course one can also introduce approximate synonyms not found in the basic wordlists, since less basic words are often cognate with more basic words; an obvious example is German *Hund* 'dog' = English *hound*. The probabilistic method can accommodate such comparisons most straightforwardly by adding the new item to the list in both languages. Thus in the case just mentioned we would have to add an item *Jagdhund* /yaagdhund/, *hound* /hæwnd/; and in addition to the new comparison provided by that addition, we would have to increase the number of comparisons by two ('dog' with 'hound' in both directions). Such a solution is very realistic, because it shows clearly that any addition of further lexical information increases the number of possible comparisons and the potential for chance resemblances.

To be sure, just how serious the difficulty becomes depends directly on how many cross-comparisons are admitted; if they are kept within reasonable bounds it should still be possible to demonstrate the connection between two languages, provided that their relationship is not very remote.[56] But it is important to remember that admitting comparisons between non-synonyms cannot make it easier to demonstrate the relationship of two languages by the probabilistic method; it can only make it more difficult to do so.

For the comparative method, however, the comparison of non-synonyms is an advantage, since it potentially increases the number of discoverable cognates. Once again, though a probabilistic demonstration of relationship remains necessary, the comparative method allows us to extend our investigation further with confidence.

8. Inexact sound matchings.

In comparing related languages we must often deal with conditioned splits in the phonemes of the protolanguage, which cause cognate words reflecting a single protophoneme to exhibit several different sound correspondences. The effects of this phenomenon on the probabilistic method are sometimes trivial. For example, in the comparison of English and German initial consonants in section 4 both the matching /s/ : /z/ and the matching /s/ : /š/ reflect Proto-Germanic *s; but in spite of the fact that the original unitary sound correspondence has been fragmented, both the fragments are still significantly frequent. On the other hand, in the comparison of remotely related languages the total number of cognates may be so low that none of the matchings resulting from such a split is common enough to make a statistical impact (indeed, some may be unique). The only way we can cope with this situation in probabilistic comparisons is to group together as a "single consonant" all the consonants of a language that might have resulted from such a phonemic split.[57] It is therefore reasonable to ask how it would affect the probabilistic method if we counted matchings between families of phonetically similar sounds as single matchings (potentially reflecting single protophonemes).

---

[56] I have found by experiment that it is still possible to demonstrate the relationship of English and Latin using the Swadesh hundred-word list even if all fifty cross-comparisons suggested above are allowed. The evidence appears somewhat weaker, though; for example, the number of the initial-consonant matching Ø : Ø no longer falls in the 99th percentile of its expected chance range.

[57] OSWALT 1970:118-20 employs a similar procedure, though the details differ and he puts it to very different use.

The mathematical consequences of this approach are easy to demonstrate with a comparison of English and Navajo initial consonants, since the number of different stem-initials in the Navajo list is unusually large. For the sake of the experiment, let us group the Navajo initials together as follows:
all nonnasal nonsibilant nonlateral apicals (d, t, t') together as "T";
all laterals (l, ł, ƛ, ƛ, ƛ') together as "L";
all sibilant alveolars (z, s, ʒ, c, c') together as "S";
all palatoalveolars (ž, š, ǯ, č, č') together as "Š";
all velars (γ, g, k, k') together as "K".
There seems to be no reason why we should not group the English initials in the same way, namely:
all nonnasal labials (f, p, b) as "P";
all nonnasal nonsibilant nonlateral apicals (ð, d, t) as "T";
the two velars (g, k) as "K";
the two "liquids" (r, l) as "L".
This certainly results in a greater number of recurrent matchings, and in matchings of greater frequency, as table 30 demonstrates. (Compare table 25, p. 53.)

Table 30.

Numbers found, matchings of the commoner initial consonant classes:

	Navajo S	K	T	L	n	Š	K	y	b	h
E. P	4	5	4	2	0	1	0	0	3	0
s	4	4	1	1	1	1	1	1	0	0
T	5	1	1	2	1	0	1	0	0	0
L	1	1	2	0	2	1	0	1	0	0
h	3	0	3	1	0	1	0	0	0	1
Ø	0	0	1	2	1	2	0	2	0	0
n	1	2	1	1	1	2	0	0	0	0
K	0	4	1	1	0	0	1	0	0	0
w	0	1	1	1	1	0	1	0	0	1
m	2	0	0	1	0	0	1	0	0	1

There are no additional recurrent matchings.

But this increase in the numbers of matchings found is not significant, for the following reason. The frequency of a unit such as "K" is of course the sum of the frequencies of the phonemes that belong to it; the frequencies of the word-initial units used in this comparison are the following:

English		Navajo	
P	19	S	21
s	14	K	18
T	11	T	15
L	9	L	12
h	9	n	8
Ø	8	Š	8
n	8	K	5
K	8	y	4
w	7	b	3
m	5	h	3
y	2	Ø	2
		m	1

It is these units, naturally, that must be used in computing the probabilities of chance matchings, since it is these units that actually participate in the matchings. The expected chance averages of matchings of the commoner units (i.e. their probabilities of occurrence multiplied by 100) are given in table 31.

Table 31.

Expected chance averages, matchings of the commoner initial consonant classes:

		Navajo									
		S	K	T	L	n	Š	K	y	b	h
E.	P	3.99	3.42	2.85	2.28	1.52	1.52	.95	.76	.57	.57
	s	2.94	2.52	2.1	1.68	1.12	1.12	.7	.56	.42	.42
	T	2.31	1.98	1.65	1.32	.88	.88	.55	.44	.33	.33
	L	1.89	1.62	1.35	1.08	.72	.72	.45	.36	.27	.27
	h	1.89	1.62	1.35	1.08	.72	.72	.45	.36	.27	.27
	Ø	1.68	1.44	1.2	.96	.64	.64	.4	.32	.24	.24
	n	1.68	1.44	1.2	.96	.64	.64	.4	.32	.24	.24
	K	1.68	1.44	1.2	.96	.64	.64	.4	.32	.24	.24
	w	1.47	1.26	1.05	.84	.56	.56	.35	.28	.21	.21
	m	1.05	.9	.75	.6	.4	.4	.25	.2	.15	.15

Even a cursory comparison of tables 30 and 31 will show how closely their numbers resemble each other. In fact, not one of the numbers of matchings found is in the 99th percentile of the relevant range of chance matchings, and most are around the middle of their expected ranges.

Thus admitting inexact phonological matchings does not make it easier to demonstrate a relationship between languages; at best it should not change the mathematics of the comparison at all. I say "at best" because it seems clear that the use of approximate matchings might actually obscure a real relationship in the following way. Consider again the comparison of English and Latin initial consonants, in which English /f/ clearly corresponds to Latin /p/, while English /b/ and Latin /f/ have no consistent correspondents in the hundred-word list (and English /p/ and Latin /b/ are too rare to demonstrate anything). The matching of /f/ with /p/ is significantly frequent because there is little random "noise" involved, i.e. relatively few cases in which English /f/ or Latin /p/ matches anything else. If all the nonnasal labials of each language are taken together as a single initial-consonant category for the purposes of comparison, the amount of noise obscuring the /f/ : /p/ correspondence increases greatly; instead of four cases of /f/ : /p/, a matching of probability .0056, we have four cases of /P/ : /P/ (it happens that there are no other matchings of nonnasal labials—see table 18, pp. 41-2), a matching of probability .0247, and the four examples of the new matching are nowhere near the 99th percentile of their expected chance range (see table 1, p. 9). It would seem that failure to demand exact matchings can obliterate much of the real probabilistic evidence for linguistic relationships.

The comparative method, which is far more exact, does not "lump" matchings in this counterproductive fashion; for further discussion the reader should consult the standard works (e.g. MEILLET 1925 and HOENIGSWALD 1960).

9. Multilateral comparisons.

Finally, we need to investigate how the mathematical proof of nonrandom similarity (and thus of linguistic relationship) is affected if we attempt to compare vocabularies of several languages at once. This is important and timely because such multilateral comparisons have been proposed as a valuable new method in comparative linguistics (GREENBERG 1987:25 ff.).

Let us return to the first artificial example of this paper, in which I constructed fifteen hundred-word "vocabularies", each containing twenty "words beginning with *t* " (see the discussion in section 1, pp. 10-12, with tables 2 through 4). If, instead of asking how many "*t* : *t* matchings" are found in each pairwise comparison of those lists, we ask how many lists contain *t* in each "meaning" (i.e. in each numbered position), we can construct table 32 (p. 72).

Table 32.

01 EG	26 ACHL	51 ACELNO	76 BDGHJKO
02 ABO	27 CGHJ	52 BCGH	77 DMO
03 ADFN	28 AGH	53 CD	78 GHM
04 AC	29 ABEFGJ	54 DFIJK	79 L
05 —	30 EIJKM	55 CLO	80 GNO
06 BJ	31 D	56 DIK	81 ILM
07 C	32 GJ	57 CN	82 AFHIN
08 —	33 BO	58 BMN	83 IMN
09 IM	34 JM	59 ACDE	84 BL
10 H	35 F	60 EIO	85 AN
11 DEJL	36 G	61 FGIJ	86 BJ
12 ADH	37 J	62 AFL	87 AGK
13 BI	38 HO	63 KM	88 ABKLNO
14 AEFM	39 IKM	64 GHN	89 DGIK
15 F	40 EFIK	65 G	90 BC
16 DFIO	41 EHJ	66 FLNO	91 DEFHKM
17 HJLO	42 O	67 —	92 L
18 O	43 FI	68 —	93 GHNO
19 AEIJKLN	44 ABDFKN	69 BCFJ	94 E
20 CDIM	45 AE	70 BDHN	95 BDMO
21 DKM	46 FM	71 FGJN	96 HLO
22 BCEIKM	47 CDE	72 HI	97 CGHK
23 EFGLM	48 L	73 HKN	98 ABEL
24 EFK	49 CNO	74 BCKL	99 GJKO
25 JN	50 ABCIJMN	75 CDELM	100 L

Observe that about four-fifths of the "words" in this set of comparative vocabularies "begin with *t*" in at least two of the languages, and three-fifths "begin with *t*" in three or more of the languages! The exact numbers are as follows:

no. of lists showing "*t*" in an item	no. of "vocabulary items"
0	4
1	15
2	21
3	23
4	23
5	5
6	6
7	3

From a commonsense viewpoint these are startling results; after all, the "languages" in question are necessarily unrelated, since they are all artificial constructs, and the distribution of "word-initial *t*" in each list is random.

But it is easy to see why recurrent matchings are so common in multiple-list comparisons if we consider the effect of such comparisons on the probability that *pairwise* matchings will appear by chance. In the example under discussion, the probability of a "*t* : *t* matching" appearing in any particular word-comparison when two lists are compared is .04, and since the list is 100 words long we expect an average of four such matchings in a single list-comparison. But if we add a third list the number of possible pairwise comparisons is tripled (list A with list B, B with C, and A with C); in effect we then have 300 word-pairs, and the expected average number of "*t* : *t* matchings" rises to 12. The addition of a fourth list raises the number of possible pairwise comparisons to six and the expected average to 24, and so on. The expected chance averages for up to fifteen lists are given in table 33 (p. 74).[57a]

[57a] The probability that at least one "*t* : *t* matching" will appear in a given meaning when a given number of lists are compared is quite different (and less directly relevant to the problem at hand). That probability can be calculated by the formula $1 - .96^n$, where n is the number of pairwise list-comparisons that can be made (e.g. six when four lists are compared, in which case the probability is $1 - .96^6 = 1 - .7828 = .2172$).

Table 33.

no. of lists	no. of pairwise comparisons	exp. chance average of "*t* : *t*"
2	1	4
3	3	12
4	6	24
5	10	40
6	15	60
7	21	84
8	28	112
9	36	144
10	45	180
11	55	220
12	66	264
13	78	312
14	91	364
15	105	420

Note that if we compare eight or more lists simultaneously we will find an average of more than one pairwise "*t* : *t* matching" per numbered vocabulary item by chance alone. Since I have compared fifteen lists, we ought to find approximately 420 such pairwise matchings, and in fact there are 431. The distribution of "*t* -initial" items and matchings is given in table 34.

Table 34.

no. of lists with "*t*" in a #'d item	no. of pairwise mtchgs / item	no. of items	
0	0	4	
1	0	15	
2	1	21	1 x 21 = 21
3	3	23	3 x 23 = 69
4	6	23	6 x 23 = 138
5	10	5	10 x 5 = 50
6	15	6	15 x 6 = 90
7	21	3	21 x 3 = 63
			total 431

This is a familiar type of distribution, and that should not be surprising. In effect, we are seeking the probability that a "*t* -initial word" will appear by chance N times in fifteen "tries" (since there are fifteen lists), given that the probability of such an appearance is .2 (since there are twenty such words in each hundred-word list). The relevant binomial distribution is given in table 35, and since we have performed the fifteen-list "experiment" 100 times (once for each numbered position of the lists) the numbers of tables 34 and 35 are directly comparable.

Table 35.

no. of lists showing *t*	% of vocabulary items	cumulative %
0	3.52	3.52
1	13.19	16.71
2	23.09	39.8
3	25.01	64.81
4	18.76	83.57
5	10.32	93.89
6	4.3	98.19
7	1.38	99.57

The implications of this binomial distribution are no different from those of any other, and they translate into practical terms in the most straightforward way: if we are comparing vocabulary lists from fifteen languages (none of which exhibits an obvious similarity to any other), and if the probability of a given phoneme appearing in a given phonotactic position in each of the lists is .2,[58] then if we want to assert with 99% probability of correctness that a matching involving that phoneme in that position is not the result of random chance, we must demand that the matching involve eight or more of the lists. The same calculation can be performed for sounds of different probabilities of occurrence and for different numbers of lists to be compared, and in general the results are easily predictable: we will need to demand that a matching involve fewer lists if the probability of occurrence of the sound(s) in each list is less, and we will need to demand that it involve more lists if more lists are compared. The details can be worked out by doing the relevant calculations.

[58] Of course the phoneme in question need not be the same in each list.

The methodological consequences of these facts should be clear. Because random chance gives rise to so many recurrent matchings involving so many lists in multilateral comparisons, overwhelming evidence would be required to demonstrate that the similarities between the languages in question were greater than could have arisen by chance alone. Indeed, it seems clear that the method of multilateral comparison could demonstrate that a set of languages are related only if that relationship were already obvious! Far from facilitating demonstrations of language relationship, multilateral comparison gratuitously introduces massive obstacles.

Because of the extravagant claims which GREENBERG 1987 makes for a methodology of multilateral comparison, it is important to emphasize that most similarities found through multilateral comparison can easily be the result of chance. If Greenberg had published all the data on which his language classification is based, we could test his findings by the probabilistic method outlined here to determine whether any of the interlinguistic similarities he has found are likely to be the results of nonrandom factors. In the absence of a full collection of data, we can only try to estimate the worth of his findings. But any reader who inspects his "Amerind Etymological Dictionary" (GREENBERG 1987:181-270) will see at once that a large majority of his "etymologies" appear in no more than three or four of the eleven major groupings of languages which he compares; and unless the correspondences he has found are very exact and the sounds involved are relatively rare in the protolanguages of the eleven subgroups, it is clear that those similarities will not be distinguishable from chance resemblances. When we add to these considerations the fact that most of those eleven protolanguages have not even been reconstructed (so far as one can tell from Greenberg's book), and the fact that most of the first-order subgroups themselves were apparently posited on the basis of multilateral comparisons without careful mathematical verification,[59] it is hard to escape the conclusion that the long-distance relationships posited in GREENBERG 1987 rest on no solid foundation. It would seem that Greenberg's research exemplifies "innumeracy" most painfully.

[59] See the discussion in CAMPBELL 1988.

10. Comparing grammatical morphemes.

Though the comparison of lexical items usually provides most of the evidence for a relationship between languages, comparison of grammatical affixes is also important, because inflectional affixes are even less likely to be replaced than basic vocabulary.[60] We must therefore ask how the probabilistic method can be applied to the comparison of these morphemes.

The principles of the method remain the same: the affixes must translate one another (so far as the grammatical structures of the languages permit), sound-matchings must be exact, and so on. But practical difficulties make the probabilistic comparison of affixes much less straightforward than that of lexemes.

One major difficulty is that most languages have too few inflectional affixes to permit a mathematically sound probabilistic comparison of inflectional affixes alone. The easiest solution to that problem is to include basic vocabulary and inflectional affixes in the same list (since the criteria for significant similarity are the same for all)—though in that case the list will probably have to be tailored to the languages under investigation, since languages differ far more in their inflectional systems than in the semantics of their basic words.

An even greater difficulty is the fact that many languages employ in the same function several different affixes,[61] none of which is clearly the "usual" alternative. Consider affixes that mark the plurality of nouns. For Navajo, Turkish, and English we can easily specify what the "normal" noun plural affix is: Navajo has no such affix; in Turkish the noun plural marker is always /-lar/ ~ /-ler/;[62] and though English uses a variety of noun plural markers, /-s/ ~ /-z/ ~ /-əz/ is overwhelmingly the most common and is productive.[63] But German uses four common plural markers:

Ø ~ /-ə/[64] (e.g. /knoxən/, pl. /knoxən-Ø/; /hunt/, pl. /hund-ə/);

Ø ~ /-ə/ with umlaut of the stressed vowel of the stem (/foogəl/, pl. /föögəl-Ø/; /baum/, pl. /boim-ə/);

---

[60] Derivational affixes do not seem to exhibit the same sort of stability.

[61] See CARSTAIRS 1984:15-6, 19-22; this is Carstairs' "Deviation II".

[62] The hyphen at the left of each alternant indicates that this affix is a suffix. The sign "~" indicates that the choice between the two alternants is made automatically on purely phonological grounds (and thus can be predicted from the shape of the word to which the suffix is added); such an automatic alternation does not amount to a real choice between alternatives, and so is *not* a case of the problem under discussion.

[63] I.e. it is the plural marker used when one must pluralize a new noun, or a noun that does not ordinarily appear in the plural.

[64] The distribution of alternants is: no affix if the noun ends in an unstressed syllable; otherwise /-ə/.

/-ər/ with umlaut of the stressed vowel of the stem (/man/, pl. /men-ər/);

/-n/ ~ /-ən/ (/vurcəl/, pl. /vurcəl-n/; /menš/, pl. /menš-ən/).

Each of these markers is used to pluralize some dozens of common, relatively basic nouns, and the assignment of a given noun to one or another of the four plural classes is largely idiosyncratic.[65] Any decision to list only one of these four noun plural markers for comparison with the markers of other languages will be arbitrary. Of course we could list all four, but that would lengthen the list and increase by that much the difficulty of finding significantly recurring matchings. The situation in Latin is similar.

Latin also introduces a further complication. While some Latin affixes have only a single function, others fulfill two or more functions simultaneously;[66] again nominal morphology provides convenient examples. Latin nouns are inflected not only for number but also for case, a category which marks the syntactic function of the noun in a clause. For consonant-stem nouns[67] the nominative singular ending is /-s/ or Ø[68] (e.g. /rādīk-s/, /homō-Ø/, /nōmen-Ø/), while the genitive singular ending is /-is/[69] (/rādīk-is/, /homin-is/, /nōmin-is/), but it would be a mistake to suppose that the /-s/ that appears in both these endings marks singularity, or that /-i-/ marks the genitive; from the fact that the nominative plural ending is /-ēs/ or /-a/ (/rādīk-ēs/, /homin-ēs/, /nōmin-a/), while that of the genitive plural is /-um/ (/rādīk-um/, /homin-um/, nōmin-um/), it can be seen that each ending is a fused unit that marks number and case together.

In fact, it is easy to find examples of inflection in which the affix is not even clearly divisible from the stem.[70] Plurals marked only by umlaut of the root vowel

---

65 Partly at one remove: membership in a plural class depends partly on the gender of the noun, but the assignment of nouns to gender classes is largely idiosyncratic.

66 See CARSTAIRS 1984, loc. cit.; this is his "Deviation III".

67 For convenience I here use the traditional term, which is more historical than synchronic. I choose this class because in it the affixes are more or less clearly divisible from the stem no matter what analysis one adopts.

68 The primary function of the nominative case is marking subjects of clauses. Whether the ending is /-s/ or Ø depends partly on the gender of the noun and partly on the final consonant of the stem.

69 The primary function of the genitive case is indicating possession; most genitives can be translated into English with "of X" (where "X" is the translation of the noun stem).

70 However, there seem to be few languages in which this is the norm; all the examples cited below are exceptional in the languages in which they occur. Whether any such cases are to be found in Latin nominal inflection depends on how the inflection of vowel-stem nominals should be analyzed. The analysis preferred in HALL 1946 and HOUSEHOLDER 1947 holds that the stems end in vowels (even synchronically—no one doubts that they once did); thus the o-stem nom./acc. sg. /kollum/, for example, is morphophonemically //kollo-m//, while gen. pl. /kollōrum/ can be analyzed as //kollo-:rum// or the like (where " : " indicates vowel length). Under this hypothesis the correct analysis of gen. sg. /kollī/ and nom./acc. pl. /kolla/ is not obvious; both Hall and Householder handle such forms with phonological rules, but many of their rules are clearly ad hoc.

(e.g. English /tuwθ/, pl. /tiyθ/) are familiar examples.[71] French offers us paradigms like /šəval/ 'horse', pl. /šəvo/, in which the noun plural marker is best described as the change of stem-final /-al/ to /-o/.[72] The most extreme examples of this type of fusion are to be found in suppletive paradigms; for example, though the contrast between English /ar/ and /wər/ is clearly present vs. past tense, there is no identifiable marker of tense in either form. For those who wish to identify and isolate affixes in order to compare them, these cases pose a particularly intractable problem.

But in spite of these difficulties it is to our advantage to try to include at least a few inflectional affixes in our comparative lists, since the likelihood that they will aid in the demonstration of language relationships is relatively great.

Moreover, in every language there are at least a few free-standing words whose meaning is largely grammatical; pronouns, prepositions (or postpositions), and some adverbs (e.g. negatives) typically belong to this class. Some of these words are not particularly stable over time, but first person, second person, and interrogative pronouns are replaced notoriously seldom.[73] It therefore seems reasonable to accord extra weight to a recurrent matching that appears in such a pronoun, though it is not at all clear how its unusual importance could be quantified in a way that is not ad hoc.

The facts discussed in this section offer prospects for the refinement and expansion of the probabilistic method, though they do not alter its character or affect its importance.

In any case the stem vowel and the ending have been fused and are difficult to separate—if the overall analysis is correct. But CARSTAIRS 1984:174-5 finds this analysis implausible, and on pp. 152-3 he adopts the alternative hypothesis that the original stem vowels have become part of the case-and-number endings in classical Latin. Under his analysis the affixes are neatly segmentable.

[71] Unless we wish to assert that the primary plural affix is Ø and the umlaut is an ancillary marker of plurality. Such an analysis works well for the German cases noted above because it fits easily into a more comprehensive analysis of the system as a whole; for English it seems much less plausible.

[72] Note that the sequence /-al/ is unquestionably part of the stem; we cannot segment the singular form as /šəv-al/, since neither part can be shown to have any function.

[73] Seldom, but not never. Armenian has either replaced the inherited PIE interrogatives or altered them beyond recognition. English has replaced 2sg. *thou* with *you* (originally the plural object form). A similar process has occurred in many other European languages, though in most it is still not complete: German *du*, French *tu*, Spanish *tú*, etc. survive as "familiar" singular forms for use in special circumstances, though one addresses most interlocutors as *Sie* (originally only 3pl.), *vous* (originally only 2pl.), *usted* (apparently an allegro form of *vuestra merced*), etc. Even more striking is Vietnamese, which replaces all personal pronouns with honorific nouns in most social circumstances; see EMENEAU 1951:114-36. It is easy to imagine such a language losing its inherited personal pronouns altogether, though I do not know of any language in which that has occurred.

11. Conclusions.

The above arguments demonstrate the truth of the following statements.

(1) Because the sound-meaning relationship in language is largely arbitrary (see section 1), the distribution of sounds in vocabulary lists is effectively random, subject to the constraints on sounds within the language in question.

(2) In consequence of (1), resemblances in sound between synonymous words of different languages arise by chance according to the general laws of probability; and the chances that a given similarity will appear independently of any historical cause can be calculated according to probability theory, provided one takes into account the constraints on sounds in the languages in question.

(3) Investigation of real-language examples shows that resemblances between the basic vocabularies of languages commonly believed to be demonstrably related occur with clearly greater-than-chance frequency, while resemblances between the basic vocabularies of languages not commonly believed to be demonstrably related do not occur with greater-than-chance frequency.

(4) The use of longer wordlists and/or word-comparisons which are not semantically exact does not lead to significantly different results in such probabilistic investigations.

(5) The use of inexact sound-matchings does not make it easier to demonstrate a relationship between languages; on the contrary, it can obscure relationships which would otherwise be demonstrable by the probabilistic method.

(6) Comparison of the vocabularies of several languages at once normally yields a pervasive pattern of systematic similarities, even when the languages in question are artificial constructs (and thus necessarily unrelated). A simple application of probability theory shows that this pattern is the result of random chance. Therefore the results of the multilateral comparison of real human languages must be treated with extreme caution; of all the possible forms of comparison considered in this paper, multilateral comparison is the least reliable and the most likely to be positively misleading.

(7) The probabilistic method of investigation and the comparative method complement each other; in fact, the traditional comparative method incorporates some crucial features of the probabilistic method.

The probabilistic method of investigating putative language relationships provides a completely objective criterion of proof; indeed it provides the only such criterion of proof, since resemblances between languages do not demonstrate a linguistic relationship of any kind[74] unless it can be shown that they are probably not the result of chance. Since the burden of proof is always on those who claim to have demonstrated a previously undemonstrated linguistic relationship, it is very surprising that those who have recently tried to demonstrate connections between far-flung language families have not even addressed the question of chance resemblances. This omission calls their entire enterprise into question.

It is urgently necessary to subject all controversial "demonstrations" of language relationship to investigation by the probabilistic method, so as to prove the truth of those claims or show that they are beyond objective proof.

[74] This includes genetic relationships, borrowing of vocabulary, areal influence of one language on another, and any other type of historical connection between languages.

Appendix A. The Swadesh hundred-word lists used in this paper.

The lists are written in phonemic notation; the phonemicizations of the European languages are my own. The order of meanings is approximately that of Swadesh.

	English	German	Latin
1. I	ay	ix	ego
2. you (sg.)	yuw	zii	tū
3. we	wiy	viir	nōs
4. this (nt.)	ðis	diizəs	hok
5. that (nt.)	ðæt	das	illud
6. who	huw	veer	kwis
7. what	wət	vas	kwid
8. not	nat	nixt	nōn
9. all (pl.)	ol	alə	omnēs
10. many	meni	fiilə	multī
11. one	wən	ains	ūnus
12. two	tuw	cvai	duo
13. big	big	groos	magnus
14. long	loŋ	laŋ	longus
15. small	smol	klain	parwos
16. woman	wumən	frau	mulier
17. man	mæn	man	wir
18. human [nn]	hyuwmən	menš	homō, homin-
19. fish	fiš	fiš	piskis
20. bird	bərd	foogəl	awis
21. dog	dog	hunt, hund-	kanis
22. louse	læws	laus, lauz-	pēdikulus
23. tree	triy	baum	arbor
24. seed	siyd	zaamə	sēmen
25. leaf	liyf	blat	folium
26. root	ruwt	vurcəl	rādīks
27. bark [of tree]	bark	rində	korteks
28. skin	skin	haut	kutis
29. flesh	fleš	flaiš	karō, karn-
30. blood	bləd	bluut	sangwis, sangwin-

31. bone	bown	knoxən	os, oss-
32. fat [nn]	fæt	fet	adeps
33. egg	eg	ai	ōwom
34. horn	horn	horn	kornū
35. tail	teyl	švanc	kauda
36. feather	feðər	feedər	penna
37. hair [of head]	heyr	haar	kapillus
38. head	hed	kop̂	kaput
39. ear	iyr	oor	auris
40. eye	ay	augə	okulus
41. nose	nowz	naazə	nāsus
42. mouth	mæwθ	munt, mund-	ōs, ōr-
43. tongue	təŋ	cuŋə	lingwa
44. tooth	tuwθ	caan	dēns, dent-
45. claw	klo	klauə	ungwis
46. foot	fut	fuus	pēs, ped-
47. knee	niy	knii	genū
48. hand	hænd	hant, hand-	manus
49. neck	nek	hals, halz-	kollum
50. belly	beli	baux	wenter, wentr-
51. breast(s)	brest	brust	mamma
52. heart	hart	herc	kor, kord-
53. liver	livər	leebər	yekur
54. drink	driŋk	triŋkən	bibere
55. eat	iyt	esən	edere
56. bite	bayt	baisən	mordēre
57. hear	hiyr	höörən	audīre
58. see	siy	zeeən	widēre
59. know	now	visən	skīre
60. sleep [vb]	sliyp	šlaafən	dormīre
61. die	day	šterbən	morī
62. kill	kil	töötən	interfikere
63. swim	swim	švimən	nāre
64. fly [vb]	flay	fliigən	wolāre
65. walk	wok	laufən	ambulāre
66. come	kəm	komən	wenīre

67. lie [recline]	lay	liigən	yakēre
68. sit	sit	zicən	sedēre
69. stand	stænd	šteeən	stāre
70. give	giv	geebən	dare
71. say	sey	zaagən	dīkere
72. sun	sən	zonə	sōl
73. moon	muwn	moont, moond-	lūna
74. star	star	štern	stēlla
75. water	wotər	vasər	akwa
76. rain [nn]	reyn	reegən	pluia
77. stone	stown	štain	lapis, lapid-
78. sand	sænd	zant, zand-	harēna
79. earth	ərθ	eerdə	terra
80. cloud	klæwd	volkə	nūbēs
81. smoke	smowk	raux	fūmus
82. fire	fayər	foiər	ignis
83. ash(es)	æšəz	ašə	kinis, kiner-
84. burn [intr]	bərn	brenən	ārdēre
85. path	pæθ	p̂aat, p̂aad-	sēmita
86. mountain	mæwntən	berk, berg-	mōns, mont-
87. red	red	root	ruber, rubro-
88. green	griyn	grüün	wiridis
89. yellow	yelo	gelp, gelb-	flāwos
90. white	wayt	vais	albus
91. black	blæk	švarc	āter, ātro-
92. night	nayt	naxt	noks, nokt-
93. hot	hat	hais	kalidus
94. cold	kowld	kalt	frīgidus
95. full	ful	fol	plēnus
96. new	nuw	noi	nowos
97. good	gud	guut	bonus
98. round	ræwnd	runt, rund-	rotundus
99. dry	dray	trokən	sikkus
100. name	neym	naamə	nōmen

	Hawaiian	Navajo[75]	Turkish
1. I	au	ší	ben
2. you (sg.)	ʔoe	ni	sen
3. we (excl.)	maakou	nihí	biz
4. this	keeia	díí	bu, bun-
5. that	keelaa	ʔeii	o, on-
6. who	wai	háí	kim
7. what	aha	haʔát'ííš	ne
8. not	ʔaʔole	doo . . . da[76]	değil[77]
9. all (pl.)	apau	t'áá ʔałco	bütün
10. many	nui	ląʔí	čok, čoğ-
11. one	ʔekaahi	łaʔ	bir
12. two	lua	naaki	iki
13. big	nui	-coh	büyük[78]
14. long	loa	-neez	uzun
15. small	iki	yáží	küčük
16. woman	wahine	ʔasʒání	kadɨn
17. man	kaane	hastiin	erkek
18. human [nn]	kanaka	diné	adam
19. fish	iʔa	łóóʔ	balɨk
20. bird	manu	cídii	kuš
21. dog	ʔiilio	łééčąąʔí	köpek
22. louse	ʔuku	yaaʔ	bit
23. tree	laaʔau	cin	ağač, ağaǰ-
24. seed	ʔanoʔano	k'eelyéí	tohum
25. leaf	lau	-t'ąąʔ	yaprak
26. root	aʔa	-kéƛ'óól	kök
27. bark [of tree]	ʔili	-kášt'óóž	kabuk
28. skin	ʔili	-kágí	deri
29. flesh	ʔiʔo	-cį̨ʔ	et
30. blood	koko	dił	kan

[75] Words preceded by hyphens do not occur without inflectional prefixes.

[76] Amphiclitic.

[77] This is the negative used in nominal sentences; the verbal negative is a suffix /-ma/ ~ /-me/. Note that I have chosen the relatively abstract analysis of Turkish phonology that employs the segment /ğ/, since that analysis seems to represent the facts of Turkish phonemics and morphophonemics most accurately.

[78] Virtually all Turkish polysyllabic nominals which end in /-k/ when not suffixed actually have stems in /-ğ-/; consequently it is not necessary to note that fact for each one in the list.

31. bone	iwi	c'in	kemik
32. fat [nn]	momona	-k'ah	yağ
33. egg	hua	-yęęžii	yumurta
34. horn	kiwi	-deeˀ	boynuz
35. tail	huelo	-ceeˀ	kuyruk
36. feather	hulu	-t'aˀ	tüy
37. hair [of head]	lauoho	-ciiγaˀ	sač
38. head	poˀo	-ciiˀ	baš
39. ear	pepeiao	-ǯaaˀ	kulak
40. eye	maka	-náấˀ	göz
41. nose	ihu	-́čų́h	burun, burn-
42. mouth	waha	-zééˀ	ağɨz, ağz-
43. tongue	alelo	-cooˀ	dil
44. tooth	niho	-γooˀ	diš
45. claw	mikiˀao	-kéšgaan	tɨrnak
46. foot	waawae	-keeˀ	ayak
47. knee	kuli	-god	diz
48. hand	lima	-̀laˀ	el
49. neck	ˀaaˀi	-k'os	boyun, boyn-
50. belly	ˀoopuu	-bid	karɨn, karn-
51. breast(s)	uu	-beˀ	meme
52. heart	puˀuwai	-ǯéídíšǯool	yürek
53. liver	ake	-zid	ǰiğer
54. drink	inu	-λą́	ičmek
55. eat	ˀai	-yą́	yemek
56. bite	nahu	-γaš	ɨsɨrmak
57. hear	lohe	-c'aˀ	išitmek
58. see	ˀike	-ˀį́	görmek
59. know	ˀike	-zin	bilmek
60. sleep [vb]	moe	-γoš	uyumak
61. die	make lao	-caah	ölmek
62. kill	pepehi a make	-γé	öldürmek
63. swim	ˀau	-kǫ́ǫ́h	yüzmek
64. fly [vb]	lele	-t'ah	učmak
65. walk	hele waawae	-ááh	yürümek
66. come	hele mai	-ááh	gelmek

67. lie [recline]	moe	-tį́	yatmak
68. sit	noho	-dá	oturmak
69. stand	ku	-zį́	durmak
70. give	haaʔawi	-ʔaah[79]	vermek
71. say	ʔoolelo	-ní	demek
72. sun	laa	šá	güneš
73. moon	mahina	ʔoołǯééʔ	ay
74. star	hookuu	sǫʔ	yɨldɨz
75. water	wai	tó	su
76. rain [nn]	ua	níłcą́	yağmur
77. stone	poohaku	cé	taš
78. sand	one	séí	kum
79. earth	lepo	łeež	toprak
80. cloud	ao	k'os	bulut
81. smoke	uahi	łid	duman
82. fire	ahi	kǫʔ	ateš
83. ash(es)	lehu	łeešč'ih	kül
84. burn [intr]	ʔaa	-ƛiʔ	yanmak
85. path	ala	-tiin	yol
86. mountain	mauna	ʒił	dağ
87. red	ʔula	-čííh	kɨzɨl
88. green	ʔoomaʔomaʔo	-ƛ'iž	yešil
89. yellow	melemele	-co	sarɨ
90. white	keʔokeʔo	-gai	ak
91. black	ʔeleʔele	-žin	kara
92. night	poo	ƛ'ééʔ	geǰe
93. hot	wela	-do	sɨǰak
94. cold	anu	-k'az	soğuk
95. full	piha	-bin	dolu
96. new	hou	-́niid	yeni
97. good	maikaʔi	-t'ééh	iyi

[79] This verb actually means 'handle a compact object'; the specific meaning 'give' is expressed by prefixes. About a dozen other verbs denote the handling of objects of other shapes, each of which can mean 'give (an object of the shape in question)' when preceded by the appropriate prefixes, but 'lift', 'put down', etc., when preceded by other prefixes. A number of the other verbs in the Navajo list do not correspond exactly to the standard meanings (though none is quite so far removed as the classificatory verbs of handling); thus the verb quoted for 'lie' means 'an animate being lies', that for 'sit' implies a singular subject (there are different stems for dual and plural), that for 'kill' implies a singular object, etc.

98. round	poepoe	-́mas	yuvarlak
99. dry	maloʔo	-ceii	kuru
100. name	inoa	-́žiʔ	at, ad-

Appendix B. Randomized lists of "word-initial consonants".

The A lists contain English phonemes, the B lists Latin; in each list the order is random, but each phoneme appears exactly as often as it appears word-initially in the real English or Latin list respectively.

ref. #	A-1	A-2	A-3	B-1	B-2	B-3
1	b	Ø	b	Ø	m	m
2	t	s	k	Ø	p	w
3	t	w	b	Ø	m	Ø
4	l	l	Ø	Ø	s	w
5	s	n	p	Ø	r	l
6	f	s	g	s	Ø	m
7	Ø	l	m	p	Ø	k
8	r	b	w	f	s	n
9	b	f	f	d	w	Ø
10	h	Ø	s	d	r	s
11	Ø	Ø	f	g	d	k
12	b	w	h	y	Ø	p
13	w	h	h	p	Ø	Ø
14	m	h	b	s	n	w
15	Ø	h	d	p	m	k
16	w	w	s	Ø	Ø	s
17	m	f	Ø	w	y	w
18	k	g	l	r	t	f
19	k	s	h	Ø	w	m
20	k	n	y	k	w	Ø
21	g	s	n	s	m	r
22	l	b	s	Ø	Ø	n
23	f	h	Ø	k	s	s
24	f	h	h	Ø	k	Ø
25	s	s	f	w	d	k
26	h	k	s	Ø	n	k
27	s	f	h	f	s	s
28	k	s	w	k	Ø	Ø
29	s	s	b	k	Ø	b

30	ð	w	w	m	n	p
31	Ø	f	n	k	r	k
32	w	b	s	y	d	s
33	k	d	t	r	Ø	y
34	n	k	g	s	w	h
35	b	m	n	n	h	Ø
36	Ø	Ø	f	k	m	f
37	f	s	r	s	Ø	k
38	r	h	s	m	h	m
39	m	n	h	f	p	d
40	h	n	m	Ø	Ø	n
41	f	d	n	Ø	s	Ø
42	f	b	g	p	l	p
43	b	t	Ø	Ø	Ø	Ø
44	s	b	b	n	n	s
45	w	l	l	s	n	h
46	r	y	m	p	Ø	d
47	w	m	s	l	d	Ø
48	m	Ø	s	k	k	k
49	g	r	d	k	h	p
50	g	t	ð	r	t	l
51	f	r	b	d	m	g
52	f	k	t	s	k	t
53	s	k	t	m	k	n
54	t	w	h	b	k	p
55	h	w	l	n	p	k
56	l	h	r	s	Ø	Ø
57	m	d	t	p	Ø	Ø
58	p	n	w	Ø	l	n
59	l	r	f	w	w	Ø
60	b	n	d	m	k	m
61	Ø	s	k	l	l	w
62	b	f	l	h	p	w
63	w	s	y	w	y	p
64	t	ð	s	k	b	Ø
65	s	b	b	Ø	m	y

66	b	g	m	h	m	n
67	d	ð	r	l	s	d
68	n	Ø	f	d	p	n
69	n	l	k	m	b	s
70	s	s	b	t	Ø	d
71	h	d	s	k	g	Ø
72	d	s	n	n	k	m
73	s	l	k	b	s	r
74	n	b	Ø	l	f	p
75	d	s	n	h	k	k
76	h	m	Ø	p	f	s
77	y	y	s	Ø	f	k
78	h	b	s	Ø	s	Ø
79	w	s	Ø	m	w	n
80	s	n	s	w	n	k
81	n	Ø	t	s	k	f
82	s	g	f	n	Ø	m
83	s	r	s	n	Ø	t
84	y	Ø	b	Ø	k	h
85	n	t	Ø	n	Ø	Ø
86	s	h	f	n	Ø	k
87	n	m	w	k	d	m
88	n	h	l	Ø	k	l
89	l	t	n	f	n	b
90	t	w	h	t	s	s
91	b	n	r	Ø	l	Ø
92	s	t	w	k	Ø	Ø
93	h	b	ð	m	f	f
94	h	b	b	Ø	p	Ø
95	b	m	h	m	Ø	Ø
96	r	p	n	Ø	k	l
97	d	k	m	k	n	Ø
98	Ø	f	d	w	p	k
99	ð	f	w	d	k	d
100	Ø	f	k	k	k	r

Appendix C. Results of the comparisons of A-lists with B-lists.

I first repeat the tables given in section 3; tables for the other list comparisons follow. MATCHINGS OF LESS FREQUENT CONSONANTS WILL BE REPORTED ONLY WHEN THEY ARE RECURRENT (i.e. occur more than once).

1. Average number of matchings expected for the more frequent consonants of the A and B lists:

		B									
		Ø	k	s	m	n	p	w	d	l	f
A	s	3.08	1.96	1.26	1.12	1.12	.98	.84	.7	.56	.56
	b	2.2	1.4	.9	.8	.8	.7	.6	.5	.4	.4
	h	1.98	1.26	.81	.72	.72	.63	.54	.45	.36	.36
	Ø	1.76	1.12	.72	.64	.64	.56	.48	.4	.32	.32
	n	1.76	1.12	.72	.64	.64	.56	.48	.4	.32	.32
	f	1.76	1.12	.72	.64	.64	.56	.48	.4	.32	.32
	w	1.54	.98	.63	.56	.56	.49	.42	.35	.28	.28
	l	1.1	.7	.45	.4	.4	.35	.3	.25	.2	.2
	m	1.1	.7	.45	.4	.4	.35	.3	.25	.2	.2
	t	1.1	.7	.45	.4	.4	.35	.3	.25	.2	.2
	k	1.1	.7	.45	.4	.4	.35	.3	.25	.2	.2
	r	.88	.56	.36	.32	.32	.28	.24	.2	.16	.16
	d	.88	.56	.36	.32	.32	.28	.24	.2	.16	.16

2. Comparison of A-1 with B-1:

A-1 \ B-1	Ø	k	s	m	n	p	w	d	l	f
s	2	2	0	1	4	0	2	0	0	1
b	3	0	0	2	1	0	0	1	0	0
h	4	1	0	1	1	1	0	1	0	0
Ø	0	3	0	0	0	2	1	0	1	0
n	1	1	2	1	1	0	0	1	1	0
f	2	1	3	0	0	1	0	1	0	0
w	1	0	1	1	0	1	1	0	1	0
l	2	0	1	0	0	0	1	0	0	1
m	0	1	1	0	0	1	1	0	0	1
t	2	1	0	0	0	0	0	0	0	0
k	1	2	0	0	0	0	0	0	0	0
r	1	0	0	1	0	1	0	0	0	1
d	0	1	0	0	1	0	0	0	1	0

Additional recurrent matchings:

y : Ø 2 (expected average .44)
b : h 2 (expected average .3)
k : r 2 (expected average .15)

The observed number of k : r matchings falls in the 99th percentile of the expected range.

3. Comparison of A-1 with B-2:

	B-2									
A-1	Ø	k	s	m	n	p	w	d	l	f
s	6	1	2	1	2	0	0	1	0	0
b	3	1	0	2	0	1	1	0	1	0
h	1	0	1	0	1	2	0	0	0	2
Ø	1	1	0	2	0	1	0	1	1	0
n	1	2	0	0	0	1	1	1	0	1
f	2	2	2	1	0	0	0	0	1	0
w	2	0	0	0	1	0	1	2	0	0
l	2	0	1	0	1	0	1	0	0	0
m	1	1	0	0	1	1	0	0	0	0
t	0	1	1	1	0	1	0	0	0	0
k	2	0	0	0	0	0	2	0	0	0
r	1	1	1	0	0	0	0	0	0	0
d	0	2	1	0	1	0	0	0	0	0

No additional recurrent matchings; none in the 99th percentile.

4. Comparison of A-1 with B-3:

A-1 \ B-3	Ø	k	s	m	n	p	w	d	l	f
s	1	3	2	1	1	0	0	1	1	0
b	5	0	0	2	1	1	1	0	0	0
h	3	2	2	0	1	0	0	0	0	1
Ø	0	5	0	0	0	0	1	0	0	1
n	1	0	1	1	1	1	0	0	1	1
f	2	1	1	1	0	1	0	0	0	0
w	2	0	2	0	1	1	0	0	0	0
l	2	0	0	0	1	0	1	0	0	0
m	1	1	0	0	0	0	2	1	0	0
t	2	0	1	0	0	1	1	0	0	0
k	2	0	0	1	0	0	0	0	0	1
r	0	0	0	1	1	0	0	1	1	0
d	1	1	0	1	0	0	0	1	0	0

No additional recurrent matchings.

The number of Ø : k falls in the 99th percentile of its range.

5. Comparison of A-2 with B-1:

A-2 \ B-1	Ø	k	s	m	n	p	w	d	l	f
s	2	2	3	1	1	0	2	0	1	0
b	4	0	0	1	1	1	0	0	1	1
h	2	1	2	1	1	2	0	0	0	0
Ø	2	2	1	0	0	0	0	2	0	0
n	4	1	0	1	0	0	1	0	0	1
f	0	2	0	0	0	0	2	2	0	1
w	2	0	0	1	1	0	0	0	0	0
l	1	0	1	1	0	1	0	0	0	0
m	0	1	0	1	1	1	0	0	1	0
t	1	1	0	0	1	0	0	0	0	1
k	1	1	2	1	0	0	0	0	0	0
r	0	1	0	0	1	0	1	1	0	0
d	1	1	0	0	0	1	0	0	0	0

No additional recurrent matchings; none in the 99th percentile.

6. Comparison of A-2 with B-2:

	B-2									
A-2	Ø	k	s	m	n	p	w	d	l	f
s	5	3	0	1	0	1	2	1	1	0
b	1	0	2	1	1	1	0	1	1	2
h	3	2	1	1	1	0	0	0	0	0
Ø	0	2	0	2	0	1	0	1	0	0
n	1	1	0	0	1	1	1	0	2	0
f	0	2	1	0	0	2	1	0	0	0
w	2	1	1	1	1	1	0	0	0	0
l	1	0	2	0	1	0	0	0	0	0
m	1	0	0	0	0	0	0	2	0	1
t	3	0	0	0	1	0	0	0	0	0
k	0	2	0	0	2	0	1	0	0	0
r	1	0	0	1	0	0	1	0	0	0
d	2	0	1	0	0	0	0	0	0	0

No additional recurrent matchings.

The number of m : d falls in the 99th percentile of its range.

7. Comparison of A-2 with B-3:

A-2 \ B-3	Ø	k	s	m	n	p	w	d	l	f
s	1	3	0	3	1	1	2	1	0	0
b	2	0	2	0	2	2	0	0	0	1
h	3	2	1	1	0	0	1	0	1	0
Ø	0	2	1	1	1	0	0	0	0	2
n	2	1	0	1	2	0	0	1	1	0
f	1	2	1	0	0	0	2	1	0	0
w	1	1	2	0	0	3	0	0	0	0
l	0	1	1	0	0	0	1	0	0	0
m	3	0	1	1	0	0	0	0	0	0
t	3	0	0	0	0	0	0	0	1	0
k	1	1	0	0	1	0	0	0	0	0
r	1	0	0	0	0	1	0	0	0	0
d	3	0	0	0	0	0	0	0	0	0

No additional recurrent matchings.

The number of w : p falls in the 99th percentile of its range.

8. Comparison of A-3 with B-1:

A-3 \ B-1	Ø	k	s	m	n	p	w	d	l	f
s	5	3	0	1	1	0	1	1	1	0
b	5	1	1	0	1	0	0	1	0	0
h	2	0	0	1	0	1	0	0	0	2
Ø	2	1	0	1	1	1	1	0	1	0
n	2	1	1	0	2	0	0	0	0	1
f	0	1	0	0	2	0	2	2	0	0
w	1	3	0	1	0	0	0	1	0	1
l	1	0	1	0	1	0	0	0	0	0
m	1	1	0	0	0	2	0	0	0	0
t	0	0	2	1	0	1	0	0	0	0
k	1	1	0	1	0	0	0	0	1	0
r	1	0	2	0	0	0	0	0	1	0
d	0	1	0	1	0	1	1	0	0	0

Additional recurrent matching:

g : s 2 (expected average .27)

The number of g : s falls in the 99th percentile of its range.

9. Comparison of A-3 with B-2:

A-3 \ B-2	Ø	k	s	m	n	p	w	d	l	f
s	3	1	1	0	2	0	0	2	0	1
b	2	1	0	4	2	1	0	0	0	0
h	3	2	2	0	0	1	1	0	0	0
Ø	2	0	2	0	0	0	1	0	0	2
n	0	3	1	1	1	0	0	0	0	0
f	2	0	0	1	0	1	2	2	0	0
w	2	1	1	0	1	0	0	1	1	0
l	0	1	0	0	1	2	0	0	0	0
m	3	0	0	1	1	0	0	0	0	0
t	2	3	0	0	0	0	0	0	0	0
k	0	1	1	0	0	1	0	0	1	0
r	2	0	1	0	0	0	0	0	1	0
d	0	1	0	1	0	1	0	0	0	0

No additional recurrent matchings.

The number of b : m falls in the 99th percentile of its range.

10. Comparison of A-3 with B-3:

A-3 \ B-3	Ø	k	s	m	n	p	w	d	l	f
s	4	4	3	1	1	0	0	0	0	0
b	2	0	1	1	0	0	1	1	0	0
h	3	0	2	1	0	2	0	1	0	0
Ø	2	0	2	0	1	1	2	0	0	0
n	2	2	0	1	0	0	0	0	1	0
f	2	3	0	1	1	0	0	0	0	1
w	2	0	0	1	2	1	0	1	0	0
l	0	1	0	0	0	0	1	0	1	1
m	1	1	0	0	2	0	0	1	0	0
t	1	0	0	0	1	0	0	0	0	1
k	0	0	1	0	0	0	2	0	0	0
r	2	1	0	0	0	0	0	1	0	0
d	0	2	0	1	0	1	0	0	0	0

Additional recurrent matching:

k : r 2 (expected average .15)

The number of k : r falls in the 99th percentile of its range.

Appendix D. 200-word list, English and Latin.

In order to make this list easier to use I have alphabetized the English list of meanings.

	English	Latin
all (pl.)	ol	omnēs
and	ænd	et
animal	ænəməl	animal
ashes	æšəz	kinis, kiner-
at	æt	ad
back [nn]	bæk	tergum
bad	bæd	malus
bark [of tree]	bark	korteks
because	bikə́z	kwod
belly	beli	wenter, wentr-
big	big	magnus
bird	bərd	awis
bite	bayt	mordēre
black	blæk	āter, ātro-
blood	bləd	sangwis, sangwin-
blow [vb, wind]	blow	flāre
bone	bown	os, oss-
breast(s)	brest	mamma
breathe	briyð	spīrāre
burn [intr]	bərn	ārdēre
child	čayld	puer
claw	klo	ungwis
cloud	klæwd	nūbēs
cold	kowld	frīgidus
come	kəm	wenīre
count	kæwnt	numerāre
cut	kət	sekāre
day	dey	diēs
die	day	morī
dig	dig	fodere
dirty	dərti	sordidus

dog	dog	kanis
drink	driŋk	bibere
dry	dray	sikkus
dull	dəl	hebes, hebet-
dust	dəst	pulwis, pulwer-
ear	iyr	auris
earth	ərθ	terra
eat	iyt	edere
egg	eg	ōwom
eye	ay	okulus
fall	fol	kadere
far	far	prokul
fat [nn]	fæt	adeps
father	faðər	pater, patr-
feather	feðər	penna
few	fyuw	paukī
fight	fayt	pugnāre
fire	fayər	ignis
fish	fiš	piskis
five	fayv	kwīnkwe
flesh	fleš	karō, karn-
flow	flow	fluere
flower	flæwər	flōs, flōr-
fly [vb]	flay	wolāre
fog	fog	nebula
foot	fut	pēs, ped-
four	for	kwattuor
freeze	friyz	gelāre
fruit	fruwt	pōmum
full	ful	plēnus
give	giv	dare
good	gud	bonus
grass	græs	grāmen
green	griyn	wiridis
guts	gəts	intestīna
hair [of head]	heyr	kapillus

hand	hænd	manus
he	hiy	is
head	hed	kaput
hear	hiyr	audīre
heart	hart	kor, kord-
heavy	hevi	grawis
here	hiyr	hīk
hit	hit	ferīre
hold	howld	tenēre
horn	horn	kornū
hot	hat	kalidus
human [nn]	hyuwmən	homō, homin-
hunt [vb]	hənt	wēnārī
husband	həzbənd	marītus
I	ay	ego
ice	ays	glakiēs
if	if	sī
in	in	in
kill	kil	interfikere
knee	niy	genū
knife	nayf	kulter, kultro-
know	now	skīre
lake	leyk	lakus
laugh	læf	rīdēre
leaf	liyf	folium
left[-hand]	left	sinister, sinistro-
lie	lay	yakēre
liver	livər	yekur
long	loŋ	longus
louse	læws	pēdikulus
man	mæn	wir
many	meni	multī
moon	muwn	lūna
mother	məðər	māter, mātr-
mountain	mæwntən	mōns, mont-
mouth	mæwθ	ōs, ōr-

name	neym	nōmen
narrow	næro	angustus
near	niyr	prope
neck	nek	kollum
new	nuw	nowos
night	nayt	noks, nokt-
nose	nowz	nāsus
not	nat	nōn
now	næw	nunk
old	owld	wetus, weter-
one	wən	ūnus
other	əðər	alius
path	pæθ	sēmita
play	pley	lūdere
pull	pul	trahere
push	puš	trūdere
rain [nn]	reyn	pluia
red	red	ruber, rubro-
right[-hand]	rayt	dekster
river	rivər	flūmen
root	ruwt	rādīks
rotten	ratən	putridus
round	ræwnd	rotundus
rub	rəb	frikāre
salt	solt	sal
sand	sænd	harēna
say	sey	dīkere
scratch	skræč	skabere
sea	siy	mare
see	siy	widēre
seed	siyd	sēmen
sew	sow	suere
sharp	šarp	akūtus
short	šort	brewis
sing	siŋ	kanere
sit	sit	sedēre

skin	skin	kutis
sky	skay	kaelum
sleep	sliyp	dormīre
small	smol	parwos
smell [tr]	smel	olfakere
smoke	smowk	fūmus
smooth	smuwð	lēwis
snake	sneyk	angwis
snow	snow	niks, niw-
some (pl.)	səm	alikwī
spit	spit	spuere
split	split	findere
squeeze	skwiyz	premere
stab	stæb	fodere
stand	stænd	stāre
star	star	stēlla
stick [nn]	stik	bakulum
stone	stown	lapis, lapid-
straight	streyt	rēktus
suck	sək	sūgere
sun	sən	sōl
swell	swel	tumēre
swim	swim	nāre
tail	teyl	kauda
that (nt.)	ðæt	illud
there	ðeyr	ibi
they	ðey	eī
thick	θik	krassus
thin	θin	tenuis
think	θiŋk	kōgitāre
this (nt.)	ðis	hok
three	θriy	trēs
throw	θrow	yakere
tie	tay	ligāre
tongue	təŋ	lingwa
tooth	tuwθ	dēns, dent-

tree	triy	arbor
true	truw	wērus
two	tuw	duo
vomit	vamət	womere
walk	wok	ambulāre
wash	woš	lawāre
water	wotər	akwa
we	wiy	nōs
wet	wet	ūmidus
what	wət	kwid
white	wayt	albus
who	huw	kwis
wide	wayd	lātus
wife	wayf	uksor
wind [nn]	wind	wentus
wing	wiŋ	āla
wipe	wayp	tergēre
with	wiθ	kum
woman	wumən	mulier
woods	wudz	silwa
worm	wərm	wermis
you (sg.)	yuw	tū
you (pl.)	yuw	wōs
year	yiyr	annus
yellow	yelo	flāwos

Bibliography

BENDER 1969: Bender, Marvin L. "Chance CVC correspondences in unrelated languages." *Language* 45.519-31.

BRAINERD 1983: Brainerd, B. (ed.). *Historical linguistics*. Bochum: Brockmeyer. (= Quantitative Linguistics, Vol. 18.)

CAMPBELL 1988: Campbell, Lyle. Review of GREENBERG 1987. *Language* 64.591-615.

CARSTAIRS 1984: Carstairs, Andrew. *Constraints on allomorphy in inflexion*. Bloomington: Indiana University Linguistics Club.

EMBLETON 1986: Embleton, Sheila M. *Statistics in historical linguistics*. Bochum: Brockmeyer. (= Quantitative Linguistics, Vol. 30.)

EMENEAU 1951: Emeneau, Murray B. *Studies in Vietnamese (Annamese) grammar*. Berkeley: U. of California Press. (= U. of California Publications in Linguistics, Vol. 8.)

FODOR 1982: Fodor, István. *A fallacy of contemporary linguistics*. 4th ed. Hamburg: Buske.

GOULD 1989: Gould, Stephen Jay. *Wonderful life*. New York: Norton.

GREENBERG 1987: Greenberg, Joseph H. *Language in the Americas*. Stanford: Stanford U. Press.

HALL 1946: Hall, Robert A., Jr. "Classical Latin noun inflection." *Classical Philology* 41.84-90.

HOENIGSWALD 1960: Hoenigswald, Henry. *Language change and linguistic reconstruction*. Chicago: U. of Chicago Press.

HONY and İZ 1984: Hony, H. C., and Fahir İz. *The Oxford Turkish-English dictionary*. 3rd ed. Oxford: OUP.

HOUSEHOLDER 1947: Householder, Fred W., Jr. "A descriptive analysis of Latin declension." *Word* 3.48-58.

İZ and HONY 1978: İz, Fahir, and H. C. Hony. *The Oxford English-Turkish dictionary*. 2nd ed., revised by A. D. Alderson and Fahir İz. Oxford: OUP.

JUSTESON and STEPHENS 1980: Justeson, John S., and Laurence D. Stephens. "Chance cognation: a probabilistic model and decision procedure for historical inference." TRAUGOTT et al. 1980:37-46.

MEILLET 1925: Meillet, Antoine. *La méthode comparative en linguistique historique*. Oslo: Aschehoug.

OSWALT 1970: Oswalt, Robert L. "The detection of remote linguistic relationships." Computer Studies 3.117-29.

PAULOS 1988: Paulos, John Allen. *Innumeracy: mathematical illiteracy and its consequences.* New York: Hill and Wang.

PUKUI and ELBERT 1971: Pukui, Mary Kawena, and Samuel H. Elbert. *Hawaiian dictionary.* Honolulu: U. of Hawaii Press.

ROSS 1950: Ross, Alan S. C. "Philological probability problems." *Journal of the Royal Statistical Society, Series B (Methodological),* 12.19-59.

SHEVOROSHKIN 1989: Shevoroshkin, Vitaly (ed.). *Reconstructing languages and cultures.* Bochum: Brockmeyer.

TISCHLER 1973: Tischler, Johann. *Glottochronologie und Lexikostatistik.* Innsbruck: Innsbrucker Beiträge zur Sprachwissenschaft. (= IBS, Band 11.)

TRAUGOTT et al. 1980: Traugott, Elizabeth Closs, et al. (edd.). *Papers from the 4th International Conference on Historical Linguistics.* Amsterdam: Benjamins.

VILLEMIN 1983: Villemin, F. "Un essai de détection des origines du japonais à partir de deux méthodes statistiques." BRAINERD 1983:116-35.

WOODS, FLETCHER, and HUGHES 1986: Woods, Anthony, Paul Fletcher, and Arthur Hughes. *Statistics in language studies.* Cambridge: Cambridge U. Press.

YOUNG and MORGAN 1980: Young, Robert W., and William Morgan. *The Navajo language.* Albuquerque: U. of New Mexico Press.

www.ingramcontent.com/pod-product-compliance
Lightning Source LLC
LaVergne TN
LVHW081603100826
845153LV00004B/447

* 9 7 8 0 8 7 1 6 9 8 2 1 6 *